CRITICAL EDUCATION IN THE NEW INFORMATION AGE

Manuel Castells, Ramón Flecha,
Paulo Freire, Henry A. Giroux,
Donaldo Macedo, and Paul Willis

Introduction by Peter McLaren

ROWMAN & LITTLEFIELD PUBLISHERS, INC.
Lanham • Boulder • New York • Oxford

ROWMAN & LITTLEFIELD PUBLISHERS, INC.

Published in the United States of America
by Rowman & Littlefield Publishers, Inc.
4720 Boston Way, Lanham, Maryland 20706

12 Hid's Copse Road
Cumnor Hill, Oxford OX2 9JJ, England

British Library Cataloguing in Publication Information Available

Library of Congress Cataloging-in-Publication Data

Critical education in the new information age / Manuel Castells . . .
[et al.].
    p. cm.
   Includes bibliographical references and index.
   ISBN 0-8476-9011-3 (cloth : alk. paper). — ISBN 0-8476-9010-5
(pbk. : alk. paper)
   1. Critical pedagogy—United States. 2. Popular education—United
States. 3. Education—Social aspects—United States. I. Castells,
Manuel.
LC196.5.U6C745   1999
370.11′5—dc21   98-29543
                                                              CIP

Printed in the United States of America

♾ ™ The paper used in this publication meets the minimum requirements of
American National Standard for Information Sciences—Permanence of Paper
for Printed Library Materials, ANSI Z39.48–1992.

Contents

Introduction

Traumatizing Capital: Oppositional Pedagogies in the Age of Consent

Peter McLaren

Now I have arrived
Now I am here, present,
I the singer.
Now is the time to celebrate,
Come here and present yourself,
those who have an aching heart,
I raise my song.

Náhuatl poem, *La Jornada*, January 30, 1996

We stand at the threshold of the twenty-first century, at the crossroads of history, squinting nervously toward the horizon for some indication that past events will prefigure what will be most assuredly portentous times. Given the complexity of issues that educators, policy makers, administrators, and activists face at the dawn of the new millennium, the publication of *Critical Education in the New Information Age* could not be more timely. Its authors—Manuel Castells, Ramón Flecha, Paulo Freire, Henry A. Giroux, Donaldo Macedo, and Paul Willis— have not only embraced current educational issues with a political and moral urgency, they have also mapped these issues with a critical acumen that is grounded in the best analyses that contemporary social theory has to offer. Indeed, the efforts of these authors constitute a new development in the engagement of critical social theory with issues of educational reform and transformation. Confronted by the new world order of communications technologies, the informational society, diasporic movements linked to globalization, cultural politics connected

1

to postmodernity, and educational developments such as multiculturalism and critical pedagogy, educators of the twenty-first century face
a daunting challenge.

Critical Education in the New Information Age is designed to assist educators in navigating what sometimes amounts to a political and epistemological minefield that has resulted from contending and conflicting
discourses of educational and social reform; further, it is a volume that
speaks to new strategies of resistance and struggle demanded by the
challenge of the information age, to the development of new languages
of criticism and interpretation, and to a revolutionary praxis that refuses to compromise its commitment to the imperatives of emancipation and social justice.

When former generations stood beneath the gilded portal that
marked the beginning of the previous century, few could have predicted the spectacular (and spectacularizing) success of capitalism
throughout the globe, including this century's greatest *artiste demolis-
seur*, Karl Marx. Still fewer could have foreseen that the very success of
capital would not only pave the way for a concentration of wealth into
fewer and fewer hands but would also set the stage for the triumphant
comeback of the dark ages of extreme poverty and institute a long and
unendurable period of suffering and hopelessness for millions of the
world population. Neoliberalism—what Subcommandante Marcos of
the Ejército Zapatista de Liberación Nacional in Chiapas, Mexico, refers to as "the fourth world war," designed *lex non scripta* to eliminate
the world's minority populations—has entered an unholy alliance with
the brutal forces of imperialism and capitalist exploitation. Our modern capitalist world economy has given priority not to the furthest
reaches of human dignity but rather to the ceaseless accumulation of
capital. The new world system reflects an internationalization of culture and a worldwide division of labor that over the last several generations has exacerbated human misery. Global capitalism continues to
serve as a Malthusian plague upon the planet, eating away the very
flesh of democracy and abandoning justice to the rag and bone shop
of lost dreams. To contest the unfettering of the market has become
tantamount to an act of *lèse-majesté*. No matter what future we envi-
sion, we can rest assured that reality will keep showing us things we
do not want to see, telling us things we do not want to hear, and brush-
ing against the grain of our most sophisticated predictions and our
most impulsive predilections.

We live at a time when capitalism has become an unrepentant universal system and the global arbiter of the public good. The golden era
of postwar capitalism (the history of which is frequently distorted by
right-wing apologists, who often hide the fact that 20–40 percent of the

U.S. population lived at or below the poverty level in the early 1960s) with its sustained economic development, its technological innovation, its promise of structural equanimity, and its paramystical promise of easy and endless consumption, disappeared in the mid-1970s as part of "the United States business class's campaign to roll back working Americans' Golden Age attainments and reconcentrate wealth and power in the United States" (Street, 1998, p. 55). Since this time, capital has prided itself more and more on taking the low road of class warfare.

Particularly during the Reagan years—noted for its aura of cultural triumphalism, feel-good rhetoric, corporate gluttony, outright criminal scenarios involving the Contras, backroom dealings with Latin American military regimes, and the brutal suppression of popular revolutionary movements—hegemonic practices and regulatory forces that had undergirded postwar capitalism were dramatically destabilized. Perry Anderson remarks that the "real illumination of postmodernism" was generated by the Reagan Presidency: "unbridled *nouveau riche* display, teleprompt statecraft, boll-weevil consensus" (1998, p. 92). The palmy, halcyon days before the arrival of the new Leviathan of globalization—when liberal Keynesian policy making established at least a provisional social safety net—have been replaced by pannational structures of production and distribution and communication technologies that enable a "warp speed capitalism" to make instant worldwide financial transactions.[1] According to Paul Street, "the alternately fatalistic and celebratory chant of globalization has become a great capitalist smoke screen [that] disarms any resistance to capital and diverts us from seeing the real not-so-novel nature of U.S. capitalists' all-too-domestic assault on U.S. workers" (1998, p. 56).

The world has not witnessed Marx's assurance that the expropriators of capitalism would themselves be expropriated by the workers, and that the failure of capitalism would be brought on by the very mechanism of the capitalist process of production itself, accompanied by a revolt of the working class. The fall of the Soviet Union has further garnered for the Marxist left an undeserved dismissal by the champions of the borderless free market. U.S. citizens, who have grown chary of any perspectives that smack of socialism—such as universal health care—look askance upon the very word *Marxism*, as if it has embedded within its ontology the demon seed of totalitarianism. But it is not difficult to look beneath such accusations in order to see the system that is being defended. Samir Amin remarks:

> It is rather amusing to see managerial types who dismiss Marxism as unduly deterministic proffering this rather vulgar, absolute kind of determinism. Moreover, the social design they seek to defend with this argu-

ment, namely the market-based management of the world system, is utopian in the worst sense of the term, a reactionary, criminal utopia, doomed in any case to fall apart under the pressure of its own highly explosive charge. (1997, p. 151)

And while it is undeniable that today capitalism is flourishing more than at any time in its history, it is also true that it faces a structural crisis of unequal proportion. This structural crisis is taking place not only in the United States but also in major European countries such as France, Britain, and Germany, which have double-digit unemployment rates. Recently, thousands of jobless people in France staged sit-ins in government offices, and immigrant youths from Northern and sub-Saharan Africa clashed with police in depressed French neighborhoods, provoking voices on the right to decry the "Intifada of the suburbs," equating these depressed districts with Arab territories under Israeli occupation. Spain has an unemployment rate of more than 20 percent; and many postcommunist nations have as high as 30 percent unemployment (Petras and Polychroniou, 1996, p. 109).

The United States is more vulnerable to the ravages of globalization than many other industrialized nations, as U.S. workers now earn much less than their European and Japanese counterparts (Street, 1998). These conditions of worsening human misery have provoked Robert Brenner to remark: "If, after more than two decades of wage-cutting, tax-cutting, reductions in the growth of social expenditure, deregulation and 'sound finance,' the ever less fettered 'free market' economy is unable to perform half as well as in the 1960s, there might be some reason to question the dogma that the freer the market, the better the economic performance" (1998, p. 238). Capitalism's worldwide structural crisis is linked to the internal logic of the capitalist system itself and is manifested in overaccumulation and failure to utilize fully its productive capacity. Deindustrialization, capital flight, the ascendancy of financial and speculative capital, the retrenchment in capacity-increasing investment by the industrial magnates, the expansion of transnational circuits of migrant workers, downsizing, cost cutting, and the deproletarianized surplus labor force have created radically new social conditions throughout most of the globe. According to James Petras and Chronis Polychroniou:

The reorganization of the labor process has greatly transformed the relation between capital and labor. Capital is eliminating multiple layers of management and administration between the top executives and production workers to lower costs. The remaining managers and engineers are increasingly part of the labor force on the production floor. The differences in income, power, and prerogatives remain, but the hierarchy of production has been transformed, and the immediate managers are more integrated into the workplace. The superfluousness of the "white apron boys" in production means less waste for administrative overhead expenses. Under capitalism, this means more profit and less cost. (1996, p. 113)

Of course, these conditions cannot be seen as a refutation of Marx, but rather as vividly illustrating the contradictory character of capitalism that Marx emphasized in *Capital*. I concur with E. San Juan when he writes: "While there is no doubt that imperialism has altered in the wake of corporate globalization, the collapse of Soviet 'communism,' and the rise of new social movements (ecological, feminists, indigenous, etc.) not anticipated by revolutionaries of the last century, the most powerful analytic framework for understanding social processes and for creating feasible agencies of change remains, to my mind, the Marxist perspective and its rich, complex tradition" (1998, p. 57).

There are many reasons why history has not conspired to demonstrate the truth of Francis Fukuyama's pronouncement that the world had arrived at "the end of history" after the fall of the Berlin wall and the demise of Soviet communism. A policy adviser who served in Reagan's State Department, the neo-Hegelian Fukuyama goes on to announce, in the cadences of official rhetoric, "the end of ideology," "the ultimate triumph of Western liberal democracy," and "the unabashed victory of economic and political liberalism" (1989, p. 3). Reason and history had finally come together, supposedly for the first time, in such an orgy of unity.

Terry Eagleton points out that the myth of the "end of history" is a false form of universalism. It is false because not only is it a form of ideological imperialism but also it does not represent a form of universalism in a positive sense other than in the realm of description. In contrast, socialism consists of a necessary critique of this false universalism. Eagleton is worth repeating:

Socialists, or at least Marxists, are often hotly upbraided with being universalists. But while this is true in one sense, it is false in another. One is a socialist, among other reasons, precisely because universality *doesn't* exist at present in any positive, as opposed to merely descriptive or ideological, sense. Not everyone, as yet, enjoys freedom, happiness and justice. Part of what prevents this from coming about is precisely the false universalism which holds that it can be achieved by extending the values and liberties of a particular sector of humankind, roughly speaking Western Man, to the entire globe. The myth of the "end of history" is the complacent belief that this has now happened or is well on the way to happening. Socialism is a critique of this false universalism, not in the name of a cultural particularism which is often enough simply its other face, but in the name of the right of everyone to negotiate their own difference in terms of everyone else's. (1996, p. 118)

There are many reasons to reject Fukuyama's hypothesis outside of Eagleton's critique of its false universalism, not least of which is the continuing existence of human misery under capitalism and the important relevance of Marx's legacy. Contrary to Fukuyama's assertion, class inequalities do exist in the West and are growing. According to Paulo Freire (this volume), although its death has been proclaimed, ideology remains alive and well and still operates overwhelmingly in the interests of capital. This sentiment is cogently expressed by Doug Kellner, who notes that "we continue to live in a capitalist society, and as long as we do, Marxism will continue to be relevant. . . . As long as tremendous class inequality, human suffering, and oppression exist there is a need for critical theories such as Marxism and the visions of radical social change that the tradition has inspired" (1995, p. 26).

Loren Goldner casts these contradictions in more forceful terms:

From the South Bronx to South Central L.A., millions of ruined and stunted lives are palpable evidence that in this system, human beings exist for the "economy" instead of vice versa, and that human beings of no use to the accumulation of capital are discarded onto the social scrap heap, criminalized, and used by the system to rationalize and legitimate its own barbarism. The simultaneous coexistence of a significantly increased labor productivity and significantly lengthened work week is a flagrant demonstration, beneath and beyond the chatter of politicians, the media and academia, of the priorities of the system. (1998, p. 52)

While surely the end of history has not arrived, it does seem clear, however, that neither have we entered into Marx's realm of freedom but rather into a *posthistorie* where life has been drained of the fullness of meaning. Fukuyama's world-historical speculation offers the United States philosophically sanctioned comfort as it glides into the new millennium, one claw buried in the chest of a defeated "communism," and wings spread against the enemies of neoliberalism and the free market, or anyone seditious enough to prevent democracy from subordinating all human activity on the planet to the logic of capital accumulation. Fukuyama's triumph of liberal capitalism has not, however, freed humankind from history but rather extended the dispensation of prehistory's tempestuous reign of cruelty. Marx, it should be remembered, did not describe the overthrow of capitalism as the end of history, but rather as the end of the prehistory of human society. He famously sought the attainment of a mode of production no longer based on exploitation but one that subordinated the use of productive powers to democratically organized, collective regulation and the transcendence of class society (Callinicos, 1995). Alex Callinicos does not believe that the world has arrived at the end of history, but rather at the end "of a century that has seen plenty of 'tragic failures and defeats' suffered by the left, at a time when humankind is confronted by a globally entrenched but peculiarly regressive kind of *laissez-faire* capitalism, whose demands are likely to cause yet more misery and destruction" (1995, p. 211).

Fukuyama's cheery millennialist pronouncements celebrate the death of doom-and-gloom Marxism and the triumphant arrival of the "good news" of the bourgeois apocalypse ushered in by the democratizing impulses of the free market. Farewell to the past of which we have seen the last. We can now flush war, imperialism, and poverty down the toilet of history. The coming embourgeoisement of the global future will be about peace and prosperity once the last obstacles to capitalist expansion have been obliterated.

Challenging Fukuyama's trust in the "miracle-working powers of technoscience and the ultimate beneficence of a transnational capitalism," Patrick Brantlinger argues for "social planning on a global scale" to avoid the human misery and environmental destruction brought about by the success of transnational capitalism (1998, p. 79).

Capital has triumphed over its historical antecedents by transforming itself into *an organic system of generalized commodity production*. István Mészáros writes that "by reducing and degrading human beings to the status of mere 'costs of production' as 'necessary labor power,' capital could treat even living labor as nothing more than a 'marketable commodity,' just like any other, subjecting it to the dehumanizing determinations of economic compulsion" (1998, p. 28). Over the past several decades numerous academics, artists, and cultural workers of various stripes have looked to cultural diversity and the possibility of a subversive cultural politics to challenge the productive systems of capitalism. After all, we live in a world of global space and of commodity, capital, and labor flows that require permeable state boundaries and hybrid identities. For some, this would suggest numerous possibilities for creative alliances against cultural domination. Yet Eagleton reminds us that capitalism is able to accommodate a vast pluralism of ideas and cultural practices:

> Capitalism is the most pluralistic order history has ever known, restlessly transgressing boundaries and dismantling oppositions, pitching together diverse life-forms and continually overflowing the measure. The whole of this plurality, need one say, operates within quite stringent limits; but it

helps to explain why some postmodernists look eagerly to a hybridized future while others are persuaded that it has already arrived. (1996, p. 133)

Given the range of themes discussed in this volume—from postmodernism, to commodity fetishism, to repoliticized postmodern pedagogy—it is felicitous that its publication coincides with the 150th anniversary of two important historical events: the publication of *The Communist Manifesto* and, less well known, the signing of the Treaty of Guadaloupe Hidalgo, formally ending a two-year war between the United States and Mexico. Through this treaty, the United States "legally" acquired some 800,000 square miles of territory, stretching from Texas to California, which it had earlier seized by force. Holders of aboriginal title and sovereignty who never relinquished their powers to the government of the Mexican Republic of 1848 were displaced, and the civil rights of former Mexican citizens were not respected.

Today, we are witnessing the continued marginalization and human rights violations of native and Latino/Latina groups throughout the Southwestern United States, spearheaded by California's infamous anti-immigration legislation (currently held up in the courts), anti-affirmative action measures, and anti-bilingual education efforts: propositions 187, 209, and 227 respectively. Faced with such a cruel and unrelentingly racist scenario it is hardly surprising to learn that the United States is helping to build up the Mexican military through arms acquisitions and Pentagon training of over one thousand Mexican military officers under the pretense of stopping the flow of narcotics from Mexico to the United States. Without downplaying the reality of narco-corruption, the strategic military alliance between Mexico and the United States undoubtedly has ramifications for stepping-up the low intensity warfare against the Zapatistas in Mexico, and keeping Mexico's markets safe for U.S. investment (McLaren, 1998). While conservative politicians and growing sectors of the United States population shrillingly denounce the rise of "illegal" immigrants (primarily from Mexico) in Los Angeles and throughout the Southwestern United States, it is perniciously ironic that this influx of undocumented workers is being blamed solely on miserable economic and political conditions in the so-called Third World countries. What the politicians and the media persistently fail to report is that the root of this situation can be traced to the downgraded manufacturing sector in the United States and the growth of new low-wage jobs in the service sector where the growth industries—finance, real estate, insurance, retail trade, and business services—come equipped with low wages, weak (if any) unions, and a high proportion of part-time and female workers. These workers are more than likely to be immigrants who work for low pay, have little employment security, require few job skills and little knowledge of English (Sassen, 1998). Of course, the growing high-income professional and managerial class in major cities has also created a need for low-wage service workers—restaurant workers, residential building attendants, preparers of specialty and gourmet foods, dog walkers, errand runners, apartment cleaners, childcare providers and others who work in the informal "off the books" economy (Sassen, 1998). That these practices are linked to global economic expansion of finance capital is indisputable. What is not so easy to demonstrate are the ways in which the United States is plundering its domestic resources to finance global financial markets. As Polychroniou notes:

> The domestic economy has become a means of extracting the necessary resources to finance the global operations of capital. The elimination of high-paying industrial jobs and cuts in wages, social programs, and benefits provide the resources through which the U.S. imperial state supports the operations of finance capital overseas. The U.S. economy is, thus, shaping up as a two-tiered economy: a wealthy elite that derives its gains and benefits from the global economy and a laboring population that works at the minimum wage to support the international drive of capital. (1996, p. 61)

The anniversary of the *Communist Manifesto* is being celebrated by leftist political organs of every shape and stripe and discussed by conservative polemicists in mainstream publications such as the *Los Angeles Times*. It may seem surprising that as a way of marking the anniversary, the *Times* gave considerable space to the serious ruminations of leftist scholars such as Eric Hobsbawm (1998) and Russell Jacoby (1998). Yet in a world in which Marxism has been so thoroughly discredited by a right-wing chorus of racial disharmony, capitalist triumphalism, and political opportunism and in which the demonization of the former Soviet Union bulks so large, Marxism is no longer considered a threat to the minds of U.S. citizens. It is a disease to which we have become fully immunized.

What is afoot today is a direct assault on the very possibility of democracy. Globalization has placed democracy, already corrupted by its own internal contradictions, in a state of duress from which it has become impossible to free itself (see Ramón Flecha, this volume). Once considered the oxygen of democracy, capital now habitually blunts democracy, placing democracy at risk. It is clearly no longer the salvation of humanity (if it ever was) but a false prophet, a *saint de bois*. In fact, capital has transmogrified democracy into its own detritus, its most fetid form of excreta. The United States has recently witnessed ominous changes in the wake of capitalist flows: massive corporate buyouts and mergers accompanied by a steady decline in wages that are spiraling to their lowest international levels; the elimination of health insurance, pension, vacation, and other benefits; longer working hours; the restructuring of labor followed by a weakening of labor unions; the transferring of stable, industrial workers to low-paid temporary contract wage earners in the service industry; and the shrinking of long-term, large-scale capital investment.

The United States has not hesitated in toppling the governments of developing nations that have placed the economic welfare of their own people before the export of their resources to the First World. International organizations are diminishing the right of nations to curtail exploitation by capital as GATT, the UN, IMF, and World Bank "increasingly pre-empt national and local laws and standards in spheres such as health and welfare, workers' rights, environmental protection, food quality, capital flows, and ownership" (Teeple, 1995, p. 123). And all this is occurring at a time when consumerism has become a world addiction, when values of democracy and freedom are being replaced by the K-Marting of the American dream, when Rust Belts appear throughout the United States, and when the pain of poverty is mocked by a culture that has given capitalism a surreal face. Basketball star Michael Jordan makes more money for one Nike advertisement than the entire annual salaries of the South Asian Nike workers; William Burroughs is used as a poster boy for globalization in a Nike advertisement; economist Jeffrey Sachs, architect of "shock therapy capitalism," delivers his paean for the new world order from the hallowed halls of Harvard while announcing that sweatshops are the only hope for poor countries. The confluence of interest between big business and the counterculture has never been stronger: there is no longer any separation between cultural revolution and corporate revolution, between the business rebel and the literary rebel. How did this happen?

The orbit of capitalist rule in this century has appreciably widened. Capitalism now circles the entire globe, continuing its historical role of making the labor of the many into the wealth of the few, and leaving little outside of its agonistic theater of exploitative social relations that cannot be commodified. I make this claim without reifying either the local or the global or positing them as discrete entities. I would add that the global and the local are mutually constitutive parts of a contradictory social whole (San Juan, 1998) and that demonizing or romanticizing one at the expense of the other is a futile if not politically disabling endeavor. Eagleton captures some of the dimensions of this constitutive dilemma: "The answer to whether the world is growing more global or more local is surely a resounding yes; but these two dimensions are currently deadlocked, each pushing the other into a monstrous parody of itself, as transnational corporations which know no homeland confront ethnic nationalisms which know nothing else" (1996, p. 119). Kevin Robins describes globalization as the compression of time and space horizons and the creation of a new "global space." He defines global space as "a space of flows, and electronic space, a decentered space, a space in which frontiers and boundaries have become permeable. Within this global arena, economies and cultures are thrown into intense and immediate contact with each other—with each 'Other' (an 'Other' that is no longer simply 'out there,' but also within)" (1992, p. 318). While one antidote to globalization is local autonomy, Robins stresses that it is important not to idealize the local, since it is always relational. That is, it is no longer linked to the national but rather recast in relation to the global. Local cultures, notes Robins, are still overshadowed by national and nationalist cultures as well as the emerging world culture.

The process of globalization is often accompanied by efforts at dedemocratization, by strengthening the state against civil society, by increasing prison construction, by enlarging and strengthening police forces (the Los Angeles Board of Education recently voted in favor of equipping school police cars with twelve-gauge shotguns), and by inculcating new respect for the cultural faiths of Western business. Wealth is being transferred from the middle and working classes to the upper echelons of the corporate and financial world. According to Petras and Polychroniou,

> In the West, globalization is rapidly dividing societies into two sharply differentiated social classes in a similar fashion to the general trends in the Third World and the postcommunist societies. Simply put, the rich are getting richer and the poor are growing poorer. In 1992, the top one-fifth of U.S. families received 51.3 percent of income while the bottom one-fifth got only 6.5 percent of the income. However, there is an even greater inequality in wealth compared with income. Patterns of concentration of wealth in the United States reveals that the richest 10 percent are in possession of over 87 percent of all wealth. This phenomenon of inequality is worsening rapidly on a global level. (1996, p. 107)

The crisis within capitalism is so pronounced that some prominent social scientists publicly denounce the globalization process and signal their public support for the oppressed. For instance, on January 17, 1998, distinguished sociologists Pierre Bourdieu, Frederic Lebaron, and Gerard Mauge published the following in the French newspaper, *Le Monde*:

In the first place the undeniable relationship between unemployment rate and profit rate. The two phenomena—the exorbitant consumption of some and the misery of others—not only come together—while some get rich in their sleep, the others become poorer by the day—they are also interdependent: when the stock exchange rejoices, the unemployed suffer, the enrichment of some is linked to the pauperization of the others. Mass unemployment remains in fact the most effective tool in the hands of employers with which to impose the stagnation or lowering of wages, to push up working rhythms, to deteriorate working conditions, to increase job insecurity, to impose flexibility, to create new forms of domination in the work place and to dismantle the legal protection of workers. When the enterprises "size down," with some of the"social schemes" announced flamboyantly in the media, their investment returns rise spectacularly. When the unemployment rate falls in the US, Wall Street is depressed. In France, 1997 has been the year all records were broken on the Paris Stock Exchange. But above all, the movement of the unemployed calls into question the carefully maintained divisions between "good" and "bad" poor, between "excluded" and "unemployed," between unemployed and wage-earners. Even if one cannot equate in a mechanical way unemployment and crime, nobody can ignore today that "urban violence" has its roots in unemployment, generalized social insecurity, and mass poverty. The "exemplary" convictions of Strasbourg, the threats to reopen correctional institutions, or the suppression of family allowances to parents of trouble-makers, who allegedly have renounced their parental duties, are the hidden face of neoliberal employment policies. When will young unemployed people be obliged to accept any miserable job as Tony Blair proposes, and will the welfare state be replaced by the American styled "security state"? Because it makes us understand that any unemployed person is potentially condemned to long-term unemployment and that the long-term unemployed are potentially excluded, that exclusion from unemployment benefits means to be condemned to assistance, social aid, charity, the movement of the unemployed calls into question the division between "excluded" and "unemployed": when the unemployed are sent to the social aid office, they are deprived of their status as unemployed and they are rejected into exclusion. But above all it makes us understand that any wage-earner may lose their job at any moment, that the generalized job insecurity (especially of the young), the organized "social insecurity" of all those who live under the threat of a "social scheme," turn any wage-earner into a potential unemployed. Forceful evacuation will not evacuate "the problem." Because the cause of the unemployed is also the cause of the excluded, casual workers and wage-earners who work under the same threat. Because a moment may come, in which the reserve army of the unemployed and casual workers, which condemns to submission all those who have the provisional chance to be excluded from its ranks, will turn against those who have based their policy (oh socialism!) on a cynical confidence in the passivity of the most subdued.

The most serious symptoms of capitalist trauma under neoliberal policy directives include: job insecurity and long-term unemployment, the loss of social assistance, the pauperization of the masses and their subsequent social demonization, and a growing reliance on private charities. It is the world of Dickens and Orwell: democracy as charnel house, as a daily confrontation with mortality. But unlike Dickens, it is not only the masters of capital who are responsible for poverty but the structure of the capitalist system and the contradictions within capitalism itself.

Although many of the changes within global capitalism have been traumatic, I do not believe that globalization represents a radical rupture with the past—some powerful and uncanny shift in global capitalist relations—such that possibilities of contesting capitalism have disappeared. Capitalism is described by Ellen Meikins Wood (1995a) as the "system that dies a thousand deaths," because capitalism has historically bound all the significant ruptures of the twentieth century, from epistemological skepticism to the assault on universal truths and the unitary cohesiveness of identity. Yet even with this revelation, one must not abandon hope since the limits of historical possibility are not so narrow that we must inevitably sink into moribund pessimism. History does not float above the messy relations of everyday human existence like some kind of ectoplasmic ether, circling around Mount Olympus, waiting for direction from the gods. Nor can it be reduced to a phalanx of signifiers that can be marched through the victory arch of liberal difference, a parade of binarisms that organize social life into black/white, self/other, us/them oppositions. Rather, history is the product of causal as well as indeterminate forces that carry with them the possibility of resistance to, and a transformation of, existing structures of domination and exploitation.

Marx and Engels were among the first to recognize the revolutionary potential of the capitalist economy as well as the causal relationship between the social relations of production and the social division of labor. But their prediction that the bourgeoisie would produce their own gravediggers in the form of the proletariat has not come to pass, and historical conditions have seemingly put beyond reach the end to class society by the overthrow of capitalism. Marx and Engels were also wrong about the disappearance of the intermediate strata such as the middle class. Far from the basically self-enclosed system of internal logic that Marx wrote about in *Capital*, capitalism has become ominously totalizing. As Wood put it recently, capitalism "has penetrated just about every aspect of human life and nature itself, in ways that weren't true of so-called advanced capitalist countries as recently as two or three decades ago" (1997, p. 1). The major revolutions of the twentieth century occurred in precapitalist or undeveloped capitalist systems in which peasants and workers were able to form necessary alliances and in which imperialism was considered the highest stage of capitalism, involving competition over the division and redivision of largely a noncapitalist world. It was assumed by many leftist scholars that noncapitalist victims of imperialism would be rescued before capitalism would engulf the entire world. Rosa Luxemburg, to cite one prominent example, believed that capitalism could not exist by itself without cannibalizing itself. It needed to participate in traditional forms of precapitalist colonial warfare and struggles over territory. But today capitalism seems to survive through constant mutation, achieving its ends not so much through police state thugs and high-tech military weaponry (although these factors certainly play a part) but through its power to commodify everything in its path. Capital's ability to reproduce itself appears unstoppable, like a brakeless train crashing down a steep incline. Humanity is being dragged into the cataclysm of world capitalism.

In its headlong rush to amass vast pools of capital (and in the process colonizing the deepest recesses of our lifeworld; see Ramón Flecha, this volume), capitalism has also revealed its most raw and angry internal contradictions and the various means by which it renders as inevitable its circular and exploitative logic. The political arrogance that accompanies capitalism's success and its Panglossian promise that it can usher in the best of all possible worlds once its social safety net consisting of social programs, affirmative action, and immigrant protection services has been jettisoned, may just be what will enable us eventually to bring it down. The supposed archaism of Marxism may actually be a postconventional promise of hope.

The free market revolution driven by continuous capitalist accumulation has left the social infrastructure of the United States in tatters (not to mention other parts of the globe). And through its policies of increasing its military-industrial-financial interests, it continues to suck the lifeblood from South America and other regions of the globe. The sudden collapse of the Soviet Union in the 1990s and the shift to capitalism in Eastern Europe, brought about in part by the strains generated by the transition to the informational society (see Manuel Castells, this volume), has brought nearly five billion people into the world market. The globalization of capitalism and its political bedfellow, neoliberalism, work together to naturalize suffering, obliterate hope, and assassinate justice. The logic of privatization and free trade—wherein social labor is the means and measure of value and surplus social labor lies at the heart of profit—now shapes archetypes of citizenship, manages our perceptions of what constitutes the "good society," and creates ideological formations that produce necessary functions for capital in relation to labor. As schools continue to be financed more by corporations that function as service industries for transnational capitalism, and as bourgeois think-tank profiteerism prevails in guiding educational policy and practice, the U.S. population faces a challenging educational reality. And while liberals call for capital controls, foreign exchange controls, stimulation of growth and wages, labor rights enforcement for nations borrowing from the United States, and the removal of financial aid from banking and capital until they concede to the centrality of the wage problem and unless they insist on labor rights (Greider, 1997), very few call for the abolition of capital itself. As long as capitalist accumulation fuels educational reform, problems will simply be shifted from one domain to another in a clear case of *litem lite resolvere.*

The *locus criminis* where the concrete determinations of industrialization, corporations, markets, greed, patriarchy, and technology come together—the center where exploitation is fundamentally articulated—"is occupied by that elusive entity known as *capital*" (Kovel, 1997, p. 7). Joel Kovel argues that "capital is elusive because it cannot be singled out in isolation from anything else. It is a social relation grounded in the commodification of labor power, in which labor is subject to the law of value—a relation expressed through wage labor, surplus value extraction, and the transformation of all means of production into capital" (1977, p. 7). The insinuation of the coherence and logic of capital into everyday life remains ominously uncontested. The economic restructuring that we are witnessing today offers both new fears concerning capital's inevitability and some new possibilities for organizing against it.

An obvious explanation of the strength of the capitalist class is that its predatory power is fundamentally linked to the global commercial media system. Nature has been superseded by media culture (see Manuel Castells, this volume), as communication technologies have a direct impact on the media and on the formation of images, representations, and public opinion. New electronic technologies are reshaping the context for the production of subjectivities and the colonization of the lifeworld (see Flecha, this volume), and this clearly has implications for the structuring of identities among our youth (see Henry A. Giroux, this volume). It also has implications for private and public surveillance of individuals and groups. Ex-CIA agents are being hired by transnational corporations for their expertise in "electronic countermeasures" and corporate spying that employ such devices as "burst bugs" (that can record hours of ordinary conversation and transmit them to remote receivers in a two-second burst), laser microphones (that reconstruct conversations taking place inside from minute vibrations of window panes) and gadgets such as the Tempest (that uses faint electromagnetic radiation emitted by a computer monitor to reproduce what was on the screen). We have entered a new era of high-tech class warfare. Profits for the rich provide the ethical warrant while democracy and protection for the poor and the most vulnerable are, as they say, unaffordable. A few blocks away from where I live The Spy Shop in West Hollywood does a brisk business with gossip columnists, private investigators, Peeping Toms, and corporate barons, selling the latest devices for industrial and personal espionage. We have arrived at an informational society that reflects a tight interdependency between its social, political, and economic spheres (Castells, this volume). The corporate takeover of the Delphic oracle by the global media barons and their establishment media outlets ensure a spin on world events that will promote a future tilted toward corporate viewpoints and hospitable to the interests of business owners, not workers. As the corporate technoelite (with Brain Lord Bill Gates at the helm) and high priests of the information revolution claim that the knowledge industry engulfing the globe via cyberspace will break down power concentrations and thus clear important paths for democracy, their unwillingness to consider a world freed from capital sets severe limits on our reentry into a world of equitable social relations.

Amid the cyberhype of the postmodern informational economy, where we are informed that an end to labor and political economy has occurred, we ignore the fact that the digital workplace (which has its own set of problems) is not supplanting the menial jobs awaiting millions of people in the foreseeable future (McNally, 1998). It remains the case that many countries are excluded from the new informational society (see Castells, this volume). Further, there exists a structural logic embedded within the informational society that leads to forms of domination (i.e., the relationship of economic units to particular informational flows in the overall system of informational networks; see Castells, this volume). While there has been a great deal of talk about new communications technologies helping to create new jobs and facilitating the expansion and deepening of democracy, it often is the case that such electronic information systems merely "extend and widen the scope and increase the speed of large-scale speculative movements of finance capital across the globe; they do not exist as autonomous forces defining a new high-tech or information society" (Petras and Polichroniou, 1996, p. 113). It is perhaps more accurate to view new technological apparatuses as prosthetic devices attached to financial, real estate, and insurance capital that enable "the speedy transfer of capital out of productive employment and hasten the deindustrialization of labor and the growth of rich investment bankers and low-paid service workers" (ibid., p. 114).

It is a disturbing truism that a politics that does not exist in the mass media does not exist in today's democracy (Castells, this volume). Perhaps because they are obsessively distracted by events such as the White House zippergate scandal and the Keystone Cops investigation of O. J. Simpson, the media do little to facilitate public understanding of the objective historic conditions that led to the demise of bureaucratic collectivism and state socialism in former Soviet bloc countries. Capitalist discourses are coordinated and marketed by a small number of transnational media corporations, mostly based in the United States. This is a media apparatus, according to Robert W. McChesney, "that works to advance the cause of the global market and promote commercial values, while denigrating journalism and culture not conducive to the immediate bottom line or long-run corporate interests. It is a disaster for anything but the most superficial notion of democracy—a democracy where, to paraphrase John Jay's maxim, those who own the world ought to govern it" (1997, p. 11).

Of course, the media can also work in the interests of social justice. As George Yudice argues, "there is no inherent contradiction between technological modernization and grassroots mobilization" (1998, p. 372). One need only examine the use of the internet by the Zapatistas in Chiapas to realize that the media offer tremendous oppositional potential. Yet the capacity of corporate power to overwhelm oppositional use of the media is a serious concern. According to some political theorists, global corporations have helped to transform democracy into a form of polyarchy. William Robinson is worth quoting at length:

Global capitalism is predatory and parasitic. In today's global economy, capitalism is less benign, less responsive to the interests of broad majorities around the world, and less accountable to society than ever before. Some 400 transnational corporations own two-thirds of the planet's fixed assets and control 70 percent of world trade. With the world's resources controlled by a few hundred global corporations, the life blood and the very fate of humanity is in the hands of transnational capital, which holds the power to make life and death decisions for millions of human beings. Such tremendous concentrations of economic power lead to tremendous concentrations of political power globally. Any discussion of "democracy" under such conditions becomes meaningless.

The paradox of the demise of dictatorships, "democratic transitions," and the spread of "democracy" around the world is explained by new forms of social control, and the . . . concept of democracy, the original meaning of which, the power (cratos) of the people (demos), has been disconfigured beyond recognition. What the transnational elite calls democracy is more accurately termed *polyarchy*, to borrow a concept from academia. Polyarchy is neither dictatorship nor democracy. It refers to a system in which a small group actually rules, on behalf of capital, and participation in decision-making by the majority is confined to choosing among competing elites in tightly controlled electoral processes. This "low-intensity democracy" is a form of consensual domination. Social control and domination is hegemonic, in the sense meant by Antonio Gramsci, rather than coercive. It is based less on outright repression than on diverse forms of ideological co-optation and political disempowerment made possible by the structural domination and "veto power" of global capital. (1996, pp. 20–21)

In a similar vein, Richard Brosio astutely remarks:

Organized workers in the First World countries are forced to compete with those from areas only recently sucked into the vortex of globalizing capitalism. Furthermore, supra-national organizations created by capitalism can act with a free hand; threaten disinvestment or a capital strike; narrow the policy options of national governments; and even of democratic politics itself. Organized labor had learned how to deal somewhat effectively with the central states in their own countries; however, it has not yet figured out how to play defense against the latest offensive by capital. Because of titanic (and undemocratic) economic changes, the industries that best supported working-class cultures are being destroyed. (1997, p. 22)

History's presumed failure to defang existing capitalist social relations is read, especially by the current generation, as an advertisement for capitalism's inevitability. The present refusal to take anticapitalist struggle seriously is undoubtedly due to the conventional wisdom percolating through the intelligentsia—as well as the entire North American continent—that there is no realistic alternative to the market and that the collapse of Soviet communism and the decline of Marxist parties and movements in many parts of the world have once and for all refuted Marx and his heirs. It is easy for the media to skip over the fact that Soviet communism was an overly bureaucratized and cumbersome (not to mention corrupt) form of state capitalism. As Ian Birchall remarks: " 'Socialism in one country' failed, not because it abolished the market, but because it failed to escape the world market that Marx so vividly described, a world market mediated through the arms race and international trade, which turned the workers' state into its opposite, bureaucratic and tyrannical state capitalism" (1998, p. 120). There exists a motivated amnesia surrounding historical alternatives to capitalism. Conveniently forgotten are the examples of working-class self-activity, such as the workers' democracy of the Paris Commune of

1871, the first years of the Russian Revolution, Spain in 1936–37, Hungary in 1956, the French action committees of 1968, the Chilean *cordones* of 1973, the Portuguese workers' commissions of 1974–75, the Iranian *Shoras* of 1979, and the rise of Solidarity in Poland in 1980. To recall such moments is to reclaim the prophetic meaning of the struggle for democracy.

Influential right-wing think tanks such as the American Enterprise Institute, the Cato Institute, the Competitive Enterprise Institute, the Heritage Foundation, the Hudson Institute, the Progress and Freedom Foundation, and the Washington Legal Foundation have joined forces with drug, medical device, biotechnology, and tobacco manufacturers as powerful political lobbies that argue for rolling back government regulatory powers and promoting the smooth mobility of capital. The effect of their lobbying for the most part helps to keep local citizens in a condition of social somnambulism. Daily newspaper stories across the United States advise us that the new world order is calling us to take up our rightful places in the empire of capital. Those "places" we are advised to inhabit in order to greet the future in security and comfort go by a series of names: technoburbs, edge cities, exopolises. Edge cities not only offer financial relief to corporations, which transfer to them in order to "reengineer" and free themselves from the labor unions, regulation, and tax burdens of transitional downtowns (Vanderbilt, 1997) but also cultivate rest and recreation sanctuaries where Goldschlager nights, jello shots, and karaoke can help ease tensions acquired from longer workdays, increased job insecurity, and the threat of long-term unemployment.

While U.S. political leaders still gloat over the fall of the Soviet Union, they feel little responsibility for the conditions that now exist in what Ronald Reagan once called "the evil empire." And while Western politicians dance a jig on the grave of communism, postcommunist countries in the grip of impoverishment under neoliberalism continue to be savaged by crime, prostitution, ethnic division, national and religious authoritarianism, long-term unemployment, a decline in production and consumption, foreign dictation of economic policy, and the emergence of authoritarian rule (Petras and Polychroniou, 1996). Failure of a domestic capitalist class to emerge in the East has left restoration in the hands of intermediaries for Western capitalism as well as a powerful stratum of mafia networks (ibid., pp. 103–4).

The left in general (and here we include those who work from a variety of disciplinary perspectives, from Marxism to deconstruction) has made faltering attempts to mount a serious political offensive against globalization. Terry Eagleton notes that "the left has always had an infallible knack of tearing itself apart before the political enemy could lay a glove on it" (1996, p. 122). Given the current state of the educational left in the United States, Eagleton's remark is uncomfortably apposite. The educational left finds itself without a revolutionary agenda for challenging in the classrooms of the nation the reality of capitalism and its stubborn and uncontested ability to persist as the national ideology. It is a situation in which pedagogy is progressively merging with the productive processes within advanced capitalism. Education has been reduced to a subsector of the economy, designed to create cybercitizens within a teledemocracy of fast-moving images, representations, and lifestyle choices. Capitalism has been naturalized as commonsense reality, part of nature itself, and the term *social class* has been replaced by the less antagonistic term *socioeconomic status*. It is impossible to examine education reform in the United States without taking into account continuing forces of globalization and the progressive diversion of capital into financial and speculative channels, what some call "casino capitalism on a world scale."

In fact, some might argue that critical pedagogy is already dead and can only rehearse the aesthetics of its disappearance. For the last several decades, identity politics has commanded much of the attention of the educational left. Conceptually underwritten by a poststructuralist approach that valorizes the primacy of fragmentation, exchange, pastiche, textuality, discursive incommensurability, and difference as touchstones of analysis and explanation, identity politics has helped to usher in a more nuanced understanding of how, for instance, ethnic and gender representations perform specific ideological vocations. Yet, instead of leading to the rearticulation of class with discursive formations associated with ethnicity, race, gender, and religion, among others, this trend diverts critical analysis away from the global sweep of advanced capitalism and the imperialist exploitation of the world's labor and precludes a focus on political economy in any but a reactive way. The *haute politique* of essentialist identity theorists focuses on ethnicity and gender issues so forcefully that there are no decibels left for calls for class struggle.

As of this writing there are approximately thirty-five wars occurring around the world—both within and between nation states—that have been defined by the mainstream media as struggles over ethnic, religious, or political identity (not to mention conflicts over class and race in urban centers across the United States). Although interest in postmodern critique is a majority current these days, its lack of attentiveness to class struggle will make its durability limited. Accounts that rely on postmodern identity politics for analyzing global ethnic and religious conflicts often elide an analysis of the forces most crucial in understanding these events: the juggernaut of imperial market forces and the social histories of these conflicts that link imperialism to the histories of the exploited classes and their struggles within the international division of labor. We need to be precise about this and not slide over its significance. More specifically, we need to be clear about the distinction between capitalism and the systems of intelligibility with which we attempt to understand this reality. Much of this language needs to be defetishized. Avant-garde discourse will not defeat the integral system of capitalism, which encompasses and subordinates all other systems, even if we refuse to believe that capitalism does not hold an implacable sway over us. Eagleton notes that "it is not changing one's mind which abolishes grand narratives, as though they would simply vanish if we were all to stop looking at them, but certain material transformations in advanced capitalism itself" (1996, p. 43).

In my classes at UCLA, for instance, there is an upsurge of white middle-class male students who define themselves among the most oppressed. The term "oppression" is now so broad and all encompassing that nearly every complaint imaginable is drawn into its widely flung semantic net. Oppression has been relativized and commodified such that it now includes almost everyone who suffers in some way. Here, it becomes necessary to distinguish those who are truly exploited and oppressed and those who suffer from existential anxiety. The critic Starhawk clarifies this important distinction as follows: "Oppression is what the slaves suffer, malaise is what happens to the slaveowners whose personalities are warped and whose essential humanity is necessarily undermined by their position. Malaise and oppression are both painful but they are not comparable. The necessary first step in the cure for what ails the slaveowner is to free the slaves" (cited in Welch, forthcoming).

Not only must multiple forms of oppression be identified but they must be placed within historical context (see Henry Giroux and Donaldo Macedo, this volume). While postmodernists examine such forms of oppression as sexism, racism, and homophobia, some of them believe that placing relations of production as the central oppressive structure is an example of class reductionism. Historical materialists are, for the most part, at pains to recognize multiple forms of oppression, but they view them within the overarching system of class domination and the variable discriminatory mechanisms central to capitalism as a system (Stabile, 1995). Because some postmodern theorists and their poststructuralist bedfellows operate from a theoretical terrain built upon a number of questionable assumptions (i.e., they view symbolic exchange as taking place outside the domain of value; they privilege structures of deference over structures of exploitation and relations of exchange over relations of production; they emphasize local narratives over grand narratives; they encourage the voices of the symbolically dispossessed over the transformation of existing social relations; they reduce models of reality to historical fictions; they abandon the assessment of the truth value of competing narratives; and they replace the idea that power is class-specific and historically bound with the idea that power is everywhere and nowhere), they end up advancing a philosophical commission that propagates hegemonic class rule and reestablishes the rule of the capitalist class (Wenger, 1991, 1993–94). What this has done is precisely to continue the work of reproducing class antagonisms and creating a new balance of hegemonic relations favoring dominant class interests. Carl Boggs warns that "while such postmodern diffuseness generates new space for critical discourse and oppositional movements, it simultaneously undermines formation of cohesive, politically defined communities at the societal level" (1993, p. 181). Carole Stabile summarizes the predicament of postmodernism:

> Despite its many contradictions and confusions, postmodernism does have some unifying principles: an uncritical and idealist focus on the discursive construction of the "real" . . . and a related privileging of the notion of "difference." If, in the end, we cannot point to any "real" interests that might unify "us," then the only form of political action conceivable is one based on "differences" in identity. As opposed to Marx's notion of unity in difference, or E. P. Thompson's "identity of interests," in which people share widely common interests which can be represented by political agencies, postmodernists reject any such representation in favor of particular and localized differences. (1995, p. 93)

Capitalism's presumed inevitability—and perhaps ultimate desirability—has persuaded some Marxists to redefine themselves as post-Marxists so that they might engage in a multiplicity of struggles in the creases and folds of culture. Accompanied by a sloganeering anticapitalism, many postmodernists, including poststructuralist Marxists, talk about creating "spaces" of resistance, local pockets of playful forms of dissensus, and of breaching the comfort zones of unreflective self-consciousness and commonsense rationality. More important, however, in their celebration of overdetermination, many post-Marxists deny what Barbara Epstein calls the "inherent connections between causes and effects":

> This approach is appealing when set against intellectual rigidity. It asks whether there might not be more possibilities than have been considered, more paths to explore than allowed for in existing theory. Yet skepticism is not a sufficient basis for radicalism, nor is playfulness. An intellectual practice so grounded will tend to sail off into the stratosphere—losing

any connection with actual or possible social struggles, and with the goal of egalitarian social change as a whole. Poststructuralism (whether Marxist or otherwise) is playful at its best, sectarian at worst; and the slide from one to the other can take place very quickly. Anti-essentialism is hardly the only dogma to plague the left intellectual world; but it does seem to be the leading contender today. And if those who are in positions of power and influence have clear, coherent, explicit goals, while the left understands politics as a game of escalating skeptical questioning, it is not hard to figure out who is going to prevail. (1998, p. 112)

Surely it is undeniably a good idea to follow antiessentialism in disbanding, dispersing, and displacing the terms that claim to represent us in a shared field of representations premised on the mutual imbrication of "us" and "them" that we give the term *Western identity*. Antiessentialism has, above all, enabled researchers to criticize the notion of the unsullied position of enunciation, the location of interpretation free of ideology, what Vincent Crapanzano refers to as a "lazy divinity . . . contemplating its creation in order to observe it, register it, and interpret it" (cited in Da Cunha, 1998, p. 243). Yet identity politics grounded in an antiessentialist position has not focused sufficiently on the material preconditions for liberated ethnic identities that have been undermined by the dramatic intensity of historical events erupting across the landscape of advanced capitalism. In this sense, postmodernism is a bit like retouching capitalist exploitation, airbrushing cultural representations so that their links to capitalist flows are erased. While displacing our historical selves into some new contraband identity, through a frenzied spilling over of signifiers once lashed to the pillars of conventional meanings, might reap benefits and help to soften the certainty of the dominant ideological field, such postmodern maneuvers do little to threaten material relations of production that contribute to the already hierarchically bound international division of labor. As Petras and Polychroniou warn: "Theorists of 'identity politics,' 'cultural postmodernists,' and advocates who focus on a distinct antistate ideology in the name of civil society must be firmly rejected. The state must be viewed as a major resource and lever for change. This view must be accompanied by an approach that minimizes bureaucracy and maximizes the redistribution of resources within civil society" (1996, p. 115).

Stabile is similarly concerned that identity politics more often than not serves to create militant opposition between groups as well as competing hierarchies based on oppression:

Instead of seeing the fragmentation of identities as cause for celebration, we should try to understand how identity has been transformed into a commodity for those with the capital to consume it and how the capitalist system has worked (and will continue to work) against the organization of socialist politics. In place of an identity politics that serves only to pit groups against one another in a never-ending litany of competing claims to oppression, we need a more cogent understanding of the systemic nature of oppression. We need to consider the extent to which the politics of identity represents not a challenge to, but a product of, the system, a manifestation of market segmentation and the commodification of identity produced by the globalization of capital as a world system. What appear to be oppositional strategies may very well turn out to be the symptoms of oppression. (1995, p. 107)

Woods is salutory in her warning that:

Both sides of the twentieth-century's ambiguous history—both its horrors and its wonders—have no doubt played a part in forming the postmodernist consciousness; but the horrors that have undermined the old idea of progress are less important in defining the distinctive nature of today's postmodernism than are the wonders of modern technology and the riches of consumer capitalism. Postmodernism sometimes looks like the ambiguities of capitalism as seen from the vantage point of those who enjoys its benefits more than they suffer its costs. (1995b, p. 7)

The conservative postmodernists' rejection of the authoritarianism of modernist "master" narratives and theories that attempt to understand society in its "totality" preserves the very distortions that gave rise to them. This has occurred through the postmodernists' remaindering of the leftovers of postwar humanism, the conflation of fascism with Enlightenment rationality, and the cultivation of a fabulously entrenched pessimism that celebrates the profusion of difference over that of equality in manner similar to neoliberals who celebrate the unfettered character of the market. It is not difference that should be celebrated but "the difference that makes a difference," that is, difference as understood in its contextual and historical specificity, a difference that can be understood within a larger narrative of equality and emancipation.

My own concern is directed at the danger of the governing tropes of identity politics displacing issues of class struggle. I feel this is a legitimate concern and that it needs to be addressed in ways that do not regress into a conservative Marxist anti-postmodernism or, for that matter, a poststructuralist anti-Marxism. I have grown tired of all the invitations to "mourn" the passing of Marx in favor of ushering in the postmodernist tomorrow with forms of identity politics that replace class analysis with new semiotic critiques of lifestyle shopping. Not all forms of identity politics are pro-capitalist, however, and some versions have actually enriched our conception of class. In fact, Robin D. G. Kelley argues that *"Identity politics, in other words, has always been central to working-class movements"* (1997, p. 123). My position is not a riposte to identity politics but rather a criticism of conservative post-modernism's petit-bourgeois driven movement away from a "represented exterior" of signifying practices that renders an anti-capitalist project not only unlikely but firmly inadmissible. Not withstanding the slippage between Marxist categories and poststructuralist categories, I believe that the more conservative ludic versions of postmodernist theories, in straddling uneasily the abyss between identity politics and class analysis, have relegated the category of class to an epiphenomena of race/ethnicity and gender. Perry Anderson writes that with the advent of postmodernism, oppositional politics aligned against capitalism have all but disappeared. He writes:

> The universal triumph of capital signifies more than just a defeat for all those forces once arrayed against it, although it is also that. Its deeper sense lies in the cancellation of political alternatives. Modernity comes to an end, as Jameson observes, when it loses any antonym. The possibility of other social orders was an essential horizon of modernism. Once that vanishes, something like postmodernism is in place. (1998, pp. 91–92)

While there are many good reasons to be critical of the current discourses of postmodernism, particularly those that retreat from the arena of the political, there is also a danger in jumping on the bandwagon of the current backlash against postmodernism among the left (see Giroux, this volume), including crude dismissals of any and all of the "posts" that we are witnessing from some Marxist factions. Criticisms of postmodernism are necessary but are often done at the expense of appropriating important insights. While I have taken the liberty of criticizing many of the shortcomings of certain ludic varieties of postmodernism, Henry Giroux (this volume) argues for the importance of writing the political back into postmodernism so that the relationship between modernism and postmodernism becomes dialectical, dialogical, and critical. Such a concern is sympathetic to Paulo Freire's sentiment that it is impossible to be neutral before the future (Freire, this volume). Giroux's important and necessary recasting of postmodernism as an oppositional discourse sets out to challenge modernist legislating intellectuals, who would dismiss postmodernism outright, and to reclaim postmodernism's central insights that illuminate how power is produced and circulated through cultural practices that mobilize multiple relations of subordination. Postmodernism, as Giroux cogently points out, is an indispensable tool for understanding the relationships among cultural formations, systems of intelligibility, formations of affect, and economic and political relations.

For instance, Mary Louise Pratt argues that neoliberalism needs to be understood as a cultural phenomenon as well as an economic and political intervention. In this sense, postmodernism can help examine neoliberalism in terms of how it creates

> categories of belonging, structures of possibility, forms of agency; how it seeks to reorganize the everyday; how it generates needs and conditions for fulfilling them (or not); how it creates meaningful political agendas that redefine citizenship and legitimate inequality. These dimensions are crucial to understanding the potency of the neoliberal paradigm—and also to identifying its weaknesses and fissures. . . . Do crises of agency result when the imposition of consumerism creates new desires and meanings, while economies are structurally adjusted so that only small minorities can actually act on those desires and meanings? If not, why not? (Pratt, 1998, p. 435)

Terry Eagleton—a characteristically acerbic critic of postmodernism whose blunt pronouncements frequently assail the fashionable apostasy of postmodern treatises—at least recognizes postmodernism's role in assisting the oppressed in their efforts to reclaim their voices in postmodern theaters of oppression: "Postmodernism is not . . . some sort of theoretical mistake. It is among other things the ideology of a specific historical epoch in the West, when reviled and humiliated groups are beginning to recover something of their history and self-hood. This, as I've argued, is the trend's most precious achievement" (1996, p. 121).

Similarly, Olivia Maria Gomes da Cunha recognizes that postmodernism's focus on identity politics has in many ways been productive. She writes that the shift in discourse of social activists from "consciousness raising" to "identity" has opened up cultural critique to new strategies of resistance: "The focus on identity made it possible to articulate that which cannot be articulated: the diffuse, the shapeless. At the same time, it enabled the integration of subject positions within a collective setting" (1998, p. 245). Yet, postmodernism is clearly more than the "ideology of the oppressed." It continues to be sold short when leftist critics ignore its ability to assist educators in creating pedagogies of dissent and possibility. There is surely a central place for the more oppositional forms of postmodern education to take in contesting the production, through mass schooling, of sites for the training of the global workforce. Henry Giroux (this volume) notes how postmodernism can—and must—be marshaled into the service of creating critical pedagogies that map the strategies and tactics employed by "border youth" as they take up meanings and negotiate identities in a world marked by globalization, poverty, broken families, media culture, and alienation. What Giroux brings to the table are the best insights from postmodernism linked to the best that critical modernism has to offer. Postmodern pedagogy as articulated by Giroux can become a political companion to historical materialist critiques of globalization and can provide a larger theoretical context for interrogating the ways that cultural discourses circulate and are taken up at the level of lived experience.

Donaldo Macedo (this volume) takes up this challenge by surveying the fault lines of contemporary mainstream pedagogies (what he refers to as "poisonous pedagogies") and challenging their creation and canonization of a "common culture." Macedo deftly identifies those characteristics of mainstream pedagogies that not only poison the thinking of generations of our youth but assassinate their hopes and dreams of a better future by distorting their understanding of world history and creating epistemological conditions that reinscribe disinformation. Macedo pinpoints the dangers of education within a neoliberal democracy. A similar sentiment is reflected in the words of Subcommandante Marcos, who warns that "a new lie is being sold to us as history. The lie of the defeat of hope, the lie of the defeat of dignity, the lie of the defeat of humanity. The mirror of power offers us an equilibrium: the lie of the victory of cynicism, the lie of the victory of civility, the lie of the victory of neoliberalism" (*La Jornada*, January 30, 1996).

Ramón Flecha (this volume) argues for a pedagogy based on a communicative perspective underwritten by intersubjective dialogue. Of course, the challenge of critical pedagogy from the perspectives of Giroux, Macedo, and Flecha rests on the fundamental assumption that teachers are willing and able to undertake what Freire (in this volume) calls the practice of analyzing their practice. Freirean pedagogy stipulates the avoidance of pedagogical necrophilia and biophilia while engaging in the challenge of democratizing power.

The phenomenon of globalization is implicated in the production of transnational and diasporic cultures, especially in my home state of California, a state that Richard Walker describes as "a Frankenstein laboratory of modern hopes and failures" (1996, p. 163). California, and in particular, Los Angeles, is fertile ground for fast-track capitalist development—what some call "tycoon capitalism." California has been a state of immigrants since the Spanish conquest of the eighteenth century. Each decade's new arrivals always outnumber those born in the state. Californians can brag—and sometimes do—that their state has been built upon the greed, the avarice, and the whims of America's finest haute bourgeoisie—the Hearsts, Packards, Waltons, Gettys, Haases, Bechtels—who were experts at exploiting immigrant labor and producing much of the country's motherlode of economic surplus (Walker, 1996). Nixon's dismantling of the War on Poverty and the Great Society housing programs and Ronald Reagan's campaign to punish welfare mothers, subsidized renters, and free-lunching schoolchildren greased the tracks leading to the state's current stranglehold on the poor, clearing the political path for anti-immigrant and anti-affirmative-action campaigns, Propositions 187 and 209, respectively.

In addressing the internationalization and diasporic character of minorities in California and elsewhere, contemporary social theorists overemphasize the importance of diversity at the expense of understanding how ethnic differences become classed, racialized, and gendered. A politics of difference can often occlude the structural exploitation of capitalism. For instance, Arif Dirlik suggests that there exists a complicity between post-colonist literature and the ideology of global capitalism. He notes that

> A major reason for this complicity is the inability or the unwillingness of postcolonial intellectuals to offer a historical account for the phenomenon of postcoloniality, and of its relationship to the broader structures of contemporary life, especially the structures of capital, which is rendered impossible by the repudiation of structures and foundational categories in the postcolonial argument. There is, however, a further, and less invisible, problem. The postcolonial argument takes as its point of departure the representation of culture and politics from the margins, from diasporic situations, and the perspectives of the disenfranchised, to question the homogenizing claims of power (Eurocentric, national, ethnic, class) to culture. What it neglects to confront with any measure of seriousness is the fact that not all marginality is equally marginal, that there is a world of difference between culture written from the perspectives of oppressed groups (some of them terminally), and culture written from the perspectives of diasporic (or settler colonial) intellectuals located in First World institutions of cultural power (or managements of transnational corporations), who may be writing from the peripheries of nations or empires, but are seated in the centers of global power. The difference is, as Ahmad puts it, class. (1997, p. 176)

In a similar fashion, James Clifford points out the danger associated with contemporary theories that deflect concern away from the structural imbrication of race, class, and gender:

> We see that theories and discourses that diasporize or internationalize "minorities" can deflect attention from long-standing, structured inequalities of class and race. It is as if the problem were multinationalism—issues of translation, education, and tolerance—rather than of economic exploitation and racism. While clearly necessary, making *cultural* room for Salvadorans, Samoans, Sikhs, Haitians, or Khmers does not, of itself, produce a living wage, decent housing, or health care. Moreover, at the level of everyday social practice, cultural differences are persistently ra-

cialized, classed, and gendered. Diaspora theories need to account for these concrete, cross-cutting structures. (1997, p. 258)

The growing nationalism and white supremacy often blamed for such California race wars as the 1965 Watts riot (it should be noted that California now has a higher poverty rate than during the time of the uprising—poverty of children is 33 percent) and the 1993 Los Angeles uprising need to be rethought from the perspective of the dialectic of race and class. Richard Walker remarks that "We must . . . be careful not to lay the blame for the present recrudescence of nativism and white supremacy simply on a universal white racism, as if the high tide of Anglo-Saxonism had never receded and as if class and economy played no role in how people are dominated and denigrated" (1996, p. 177). "It is not enough," notes Walker, to "declare race the central stratifying variable. The scramble for class power and privilege has lent particular force to the suppression of contending 'races,' and the denigration of those at the bottom of the class system has gone hand in hand with racial character assassination" (ibid.). Racial conquest and class encounter was not the sole provenance of the working classes, it should be remembered, but was overwhelmingly conjugated with the practices of financiers, the petit bourgeoisie, and plantation merchants and continues today as part of a politics of political opportunism and mass disenfranchisement within an elite war of position (ibid.).

We need to develop a revolutionary multiculturalism that shares much in common with the pedagogies developed (in this volume) by Giroux, Macedo, Flecha, and Freire. A revolutionary multicultural pedagogy challenges educators to develop a concept of unity and difference that reconfigures the meaning of difference as political mobilization rather than cultural authenticity (see Flecha). In raising the *quaestio vexata* of domination, it calls for rejecting pedagogical approaches based on ethnocentrism and rejecting relativism in favor of interculturalist and pluriculturalist approaches grounded in a critical utopianism (see Flecha). It also is directed at dismantling the discourses of power and privilege and social practices that have epistemically mutated into new and terrifying forms of xenophobic nationalism in which there is but one universal subject of history: the white, Anglo, heterosexual male of bourgeois privilege. In saying this, I am not arguing that Western cultures and their offspring are only and always oppressive. Here, Eagleton's admonition bears repeating: "What an insult to the working people of the West, whose labor lay at the source of those cultures, to inform them airily that they are nothing but oppressive! And how conveniently such histrionic gestures serve to reinforce forms of ethnocentrism in the so-called third world itself, thus merely exporting the beast from one sphere to another" (1996, p. 125). Yet the challenge of critical pedagogy does point to a necessary displacement of the United States as the center of analysis and to the development of a more inclusive, global perspective, one that needs to be decentered and de-Westernized (see Macedo, this volume).

We need to move beyond celebrating pluralism. We need to understand how discursive constructions of race and ethnicity are linked to economic exploitation. In other words, we need to explore how forms of ethnicity are structurally imbricated in the antinomic configuration of flexible transnational capitalism. If we are to build upon these insights in our pedagogical practices, we would do well to follow the suggestions of Paul Willis (this volume), who argues that if we wish to fully understand the process by which capital accumulation is realized through circuit and exchange, we need to examine the commodity form, what Marx refers to as a "social hieroglyph." An examination of the nature of cultural commodities can help us understand how symbols are made to connect with reality and how they shape, reflect, and refract reality. An understanding of universal commodity culture and the ubiquity of the commodity form is essential in grasping the myriad ways in which meanings exist as commodities within personal modes of production. Willis's insights complement the critical pedagogy advanced by Giroux, Macedo, and Freire when he calls for a focus on whole cultural processes fed by signs and commodities rather than an emphasis on their separate coding and decoding instances. In this way, radical educators can help their students understand how labor power is produced as a special form of commodity capable of infinite extension and adaptation and how the autonomy of commodity culture is in actuality a ruse. Despite their appearance otherwise, commodities are always connected to, and mediated by, the larger social totality.

The emerging field of critical media literacy speaks to Willis's preoccupation with cultural artifacts as commodity forms and also registers Manuel Castells' emphasis (this volume) on understanding the specific effects of the technological revolution on the social structure. The fundamental realization that guides the development of a critical media literacy as part of a critical/postmodern pedagogy is that, although the production of knowledge and social organization have enabled us as a species to live in a purely social world, we are now entering a new battleground for the political control of meaning through the skilled manipulation of messages and symbols. Educators need to understand the profound implication that informational culture poses for the future of democracy (Giroux, this volume). Teaching critically in an informational culture stipulates that students understand what is at stake in struggling for access to specific flows of knowledge or information within networks of economic exchanges.

In other words, critical pedagogy needs to establish a project of emancipation that moves beyond simply wringing concessions from existing capitalist structures and institutions. Rather, it must be centered on the transformation of property relations and the creation of a just system of appropriation and distribution of social wealth. It is not enough to adjust the foundational level of school funding to account for levels of student poverty, to propose supplemental funding for poverty and limited English proficiency, to raise local taxes to benefit schools, to demand that state governments partly subsidize low-property-value communities, or to fight for the equalization of funding generated by low-property-value districts (although these efforts surely would be a step in the right direction). I am arguing for a fundamentally broader vision based on a transformation of global economic relations—on a different economic logic, if you will—that transcends a mere reformism within existing social relations of production and international division of labor. But challenging the swaggering, gun-slinging, frontier-style economic practices of the tycoon capitalism that we are witnessing today must also be accompanied (as Giroux argues) by a powerful cultural critique that can speak forcefully to the creation of antiracist, antisexist, and antihomophobic pedagogies of liberation.

In our attempts to rethink and revise our pedagogies of liberation in light of the challenges brought on by the new informational age, we need to remember that the global options of transnational corporations are not endless and that the state is not fully external to the market and, therefore, powerless. The state still serves as a center for both managing and restructuring labor–capital relations at times of crisis and in no way has become fully fetishized. Markets do not control states in an absolute fashion, rendering them obsolete. We can struggle against the state without falling into the myth of globalization. The state can potentially be rearticulated through revolutionary praxis to serve the interests of the powerless and disenfranchised. While we may not be able to delink ourselves from the global project, we can struggle to undermine it in a "pluriverse" of important ways.

Yet, in our struggles for local autonomy we must not give up the fight for a renewed civic sphere and the essential components of this sphere: our schools. Questions that need to foreground our debates as we engage in the continuing struggle for democracy can be formulated as follows: Can a reconfigured civil society alter institutional arrangements in the interest of social justice? Can a reorganization of civil society serve as the basis for renewing the state–nation compact (Yudice, 1998, p. 372)? Can we now begin a new process of writing history from

below? The potential outcomes that follow from such questions point
to some of the hopes and promises of the struggle ahead. We need to
engage this struggle not as vanguardists or adventurists but as committed cultural workers engaged in companionable, solidarity-build-
ing strategies that will effectively change the production process, priz-
ing it away from the bourgeois elites, rather than providing grist for its
mill. In this context, social movements must play an important role in
the struggle ahead (see Flecha, this volume). As social theorist and
labor historian, Stanley Aronowitz (1981), argues, new forms of politics
need to be developed in the conflictual arenas of culture (see Giroux,
Willis, and Castells, this volume).

Critical pedagogy must recognize that identity is positionality—
what Stuart Hall calls "the point of suture between the social and the
psychic" (1997, p. 33). An identity politics that celebrates linguistically
defined positionality in language and avoids defining positionality in
terms of the state, social structures, and larger configurations of power
and privilege should be discarded. Critical pedagogy must transmute
into a contraband pedagogy, a renegade pedagogy that views identity
as a contingent articulation among class interests, social forces, and signifying practices and that replaces an essentialist logic with a theory of
otherness as a form of positivity based on notions of effectivity, belonging, and "the changing same" (Grossberg, 1997; Gilroy, 1993). A
contraband pedagogy builds upon class solidarity without ignoring
differences by conceiving alliances across race and gender as a set of
affiliations (Kelley, 1997). Identities are understood as both momentary
and historical investments in social discourse, as different positionali-
ties that you permit yourself to be subjected to, and that are imbricated
in different race, class, and gender histories that are inscribed in these
positions (Hall, 1997). Yet at the same time contraband pedagogy is at-
tentive to the ways in which the ideology of the free market has, at this
historical moment, been sutured into our daily vernacular so as to secure a particular configuration of dominant class interests.

Critical pedagogy serves, in the broadest sense, as a political herme-
neutic that guides the articulation of lived meaning within the contin-
gencies of history, according to an ethical commitment to social justice
(see Giroux and Macedo, this volume). It has constituted itself as a way
of navigating through the technologies of power created within the
contested terrains of postmodern cultures. Critical pedagogy as I am
fashioning it argues for the self-education of the working class and
struggles against alienated labor in which the worker becomes poorer
the more wealth she produces and in which the increase in the world
of commodities is directly related to the estrangement of the worker
from herself and her species-life. The strength of critical pedagogy lies

in its capacity to foster the principle of social justice and to propel this principle into the realm of hope, so that it might arch toward the future in a continuing orbit of possibility. In doing so, it offers a historical challenge to helplessness and despair. Its strength also resides in its singular ability to make resignation implausible and defeat untenable, despite the criticism launched by some that would immobilize critical pedagogy by dismissing it as "always already" trapped within a modernist voice of sovereign authority and totalizing certitude. Critical pedagogy functions as a form of critical utopianism that reveals the birth of tomorrow out of the struggle of today. Critical pedagogy must move forward into the next millennium uncompromised in its commitment to help individuals free themselves from their socially enclaved lives so that they might make themselves available to their collective imagination. Yet it needs to recognize its own provisionality, and to caution itself against prematurely bringing closure to the narrative of emancipation. The politics of the imagination upon which critical pedagogy is based also requires that we imprint our collective will on the workings of history. What the left needs is not a republic of dreamers isolated from class struggle but a contraband pedagogy, a profane pedagogy and educational brigandism for the next century, one capable of forging new tactical possibilities for pressing forward the project of social democracy and setting limits to the reign of capital. It is this unalloyed commitment to critical agency, in particular, that creates such a formidable alliance among the diverse authors of this volume, and it is what makes *Critical Education in the New Information Age* such an important resource for the challenging times ahead.

Notes

1. The regional and liberalization pacts that emerged in the past decade—the World Trade Organization, the North American Free Trade Agreement, the European Union, Latin America's Mercosur, and the recent negotiations of the Organization for Economic Cooperation and Development surrounding the Multilateral Agreement on Investment—are shaping the new world order in accordance with the most ideal investment conditions for transnational corporations. It is no secret that the GATT-WTO is subservient to the will of the transnational monopolies, promotes unilateral adjustment from the weakest nations to the strongest, occludes the issue of sustainable development, and severs the connection between economic management and political and social management (see Samir Amin, *Capitalism in the Age of Globalization*, London and New Jersey: Zed Books, 1997). Anything hindering foreign investment—i.e., rules and regulations that protect workers and jobs, public welfare, environment, culture, and domestic businesses—is dutifully removed. The World

Trade Organization (which was created on January 1, 1995, following the signing of the GATT global free trade agreement in 1994) and the International Monetary Fund both work to obtain trade concessions from those countries whose economies are in distress and to gain access to unprotected sectors of Third World economies. The WTO, the IMF, the OECD, The International Chamber of Commerce, the European Round Table of Industrialists, the Union of Industrial and Employers Confederation of Europe, the United States Council for International Business, the International Organization of Employers, the Business Council on National Issues, the World Business Council for Sustainable Development, the United Nations Commission on Trade and Development, the Business and Industry Advisory Committee, all work to ensure market control and assist transnational corporations in becoming some of the largest economies in the world. In the United States, research centers in Silicon Valley, Route 128 in Boston, the Research Triangle in North Carolina (Raleigh/Durham) and Fairfax County, Virginia, and other locations throughout the country are not only facilitating possibilities for electronic commerce, but are creating technological contexts for corporate mergers and take-overs.

Of course the philosophical architecture of neoliberalism behind all of this can be traced to the bourgeois salons of "Red Vienna" and the thinking of Frederich Von Hayek, an Austrian economist who moved to the University of Chicago and became the mentor of Milton Friedman (not to mention influencing Ronald Reagan and Margaret Thatcher). Hayek's concept of "the catallaxy" or the spontaneous relations of free economic exchange between individuals (influenced by the work of Ernst Mach and Michael Polyani) rests on the notion that there exists no connection between human intention and social outcome and that the outcome of all human activity is essentially haphazard. This position opposes that of the critical educationalists in this volume who emphasize the sociohistorical context of economic systems and who stress the socially constituted way in which knowledge about social life might lead to revolutionary action on behalf of the oppressed. Hayek's bourgeois ideological perceptions led him to the economistic idea that culture must adjust to the economic imperatives of the marketplace. He was militantly opposed to government regulation in general, except when it came to protecting the free, unfettered functioning of the market (see Hilary Wainwright, *Arguments for a New Left: Answering the Free Market Right*, London and Cambridge: Blackwell, 1994).

References

Anderson, Perry. 1998. *The Origins of Postmodernity*. London and New York: Verso Books.

Amin, Samir. 1997. *Capitalism in the Age of Globalization*. London: Zed Books, Ltd.

Aronowitz, Stanley. 1981. *The Crisis in Historical Materialism*. South Hadley: Bergin and Garvey Publishers.

Birchall, Ian. 1998. "The Manifesto Remains a Guide." *New Politics* vol. 6, no. 4 (n.s.): 114–21.

Boggs, Carl. 1993. *Intellectuals and the Crisis of Modernity.* Albany, New York: The State University Press of New York.

Brantlinger, Patrick. 1998. "Apocalypse 2001; or, What Happens After Posthistory?" *Cultural Critique* 39: 59–83.

Brenner, Robert. 1998. "The Economics of Global Turbulence." *New Left Review* 229: 1–264.

Brosio, Richard A. 1997. "The Complexity Constructed Citizen Worker: Her/ His Centrality to the Struggle for Radical Democratic Politics and Education." *Journal of Thought* (Fall): 9–26.

Callinicos, Alex. 1995. *Theories and Narratives: Reflections on the Philosophy of History.* Durham: Duke University Press.

Clifford, James. 1997. *Routes: Travel and Translation in the Late Twentieth Century.* Cambridge: Harvard University Press.

Da Cunha, Olivia Maria Gomes. 1998. "Black Movements and the 'Politics of Identity' in Brazil." In Sonia E. Alvarez, Evelina Dagnino, and Arturo Escobar, eds., *Cultures of Politics, Politics of Culture: Re-Visioning Latin American Social Movements.* Boulder, Colo.: Westview.

Dirlik, Arif. 1997. *The Postcolonial Aura: Third World Criticism in the Age of Global Capitalism.* Boulder, Colo.: Westview.

Eagleton, Terry. 1996. *The Illusions of Postmodernism.* Oxford and Cambridge: Blackwell.

Epstein, Barbara. 1998. "Interpreting the World (Without Necessarily Changing It)." *New Politics* vol. 6, no. 4 (n.s.): 107–13.

Fukuyama, Francis. 1989. "The End of History?" *The National Interest* 16 (Summer): 3–18.

Gilroy, Paul. 1993. *The Black Atlantic.* Cambridge: Harvard University Press.

Goldner, Loren. 1998. "A Tribute to the Manifesto." *New Politics* vol. 6, no. 4 (n.s.): 48–53.

Greider, William. 1997. "Saving the Global Economy." *Nation* 265: 11–16.

Grossberg, Lawrence. 1997. *Bringing it all Back Home.* Durham and London: Duke University Press.

Hall, Stuart. 1997. "Culture and Power: Stuart Hall Interviewed by Peter Osborne and Lynne Segal." *Radical Philosophy,* vol. 86, Nov./Dec., 24–41.

Hobsbawm, Eric. 1998. "Why Read Marx?" *Los Angeles Times Book Review,* February 8.

Jacoby, Russell. 1998. "Marx Reconsidered: A Symposium." *Los Angeles Times Book Review,* February 8.

Kelley, Robin D. G. 1997. *Yo' Mama's Disfunktional!* Boston, Mass.: Beacon Press.

Kellner, Douglas. 1995. "The Obsolescence of Marxism?" In Bernd Magnus and Stephen Cullenberg, eds., *Whither Marxism? Global Crises in International Perspective.* London: Routledge.

Kovel, Joel. 1997. "The Enemy of Nature." *Monthly Review* 49: 6–14.

McChesney, Robert W. 1997. "The Global Media Giants: Nine Firms that Dominate the World." *Extra!* 10: 11–18.

McLaren, Peter. 1998. "The Pedagogy of Che Guevara." *Cultural Circles* vol. 3, 28–104.

McNally, David. 1998. "Marxism in the Age of Information." *New Politics* vol. 6, no. 4 (n.s.): 99–106.

Mészáros, István. 1998. "Globalizing Capital." *Monthly Review* 49: 27–37.

Petras, James, and Chronis Polychroniou. 1996. "Capitalist Transformation: The Relevance of and Challenges to Marxism." In Chronis Polychroniou and Harry R. Targ, eds., *Marxism Today: Essays on Capitalism, Socialism, and Strategies for Social Change.* Westport, Conn.: Praeger.

Polychroniou, Chronis. 1996. "The Political Economy of U.S. Imperialism: From Hegemony to Crisis." In Chronis Polychroniou and Harry R. Targ, eds., *Marxism Today: Essays on Capitalism, Socialism, and Strategies for Social Change.* Westport, Conn.: Praeger.

Pratt, Mary Louise. 1998. "Where To? What Next?" In Sonia E. Alvarez, Evelina Dagnino, and Arturo Escobar, eds., *Cultures of Politics, Politics of Cultures: Re-Visioning Latin American Social Movements.* Boulder, Colo.: Westview.

Robinson, William I. 1996. "Globalisation: Nine Theses on Our Epoch." *Race and Class* 38: 13–29.

Robins, Kevin. 1992. "Reading a Global Culture." In Stuart Hall, David Held, and Tony McGrew, eds., *Modernity and Its Futures.* Oxford: Polity.

San Juan, E. 1998. *Beyond Postcolonialism.* New York: St. Martin's.

Sassen, Saskia. 1998. *Globalization and Its Discontents: Essays on the New Mobility of People and Money.* New York: The New Press.

Stabile, Carol A. 1995. "Postmodernism, Feminism, and Marx: Notes from the Abyss." *Monthly Review* 47: 89–107.

Street, Paul. 1998. "The Judas Economy and the Limits of Acceptable Debate: A Critique of Wolman and Colamosca." *Monthly Review* 49: 53–59.

Teeple, Gary. 1995. *Globalization and the Decline of Social Reform.* New Jersey: Humanities Press.

Vanderbilt, Tom. 1997. "Revolt of the Nice: Edge City, Capital of the Twenty-first Century." In Thomas Frank and Matt Weiland, eds., *Commodify Your Dissent.* New York: Norton.

Walker, Richard. 1996. "California's Collision of Race and Class." *Representations* (Summer): 163–83.

Welch, Sharon D. Forthcoming. *Sweet Dreams in America: The Ethical and Spiritual Challenge of Multiculturalism.* New York: Routledge.

Wenger, Morton. 1991. "Decoding Postmodernism: The Despair of the Intellectuals and the Twilight of the Future." *Social Science Journal* 28: 391–407.

———. 1993–94. "Idealism Redux: The Class-Historical Truth of Postmodernism." *Critical Sociology* 20: 53–78.

Wood, Ellen Meikins. 1995a. *Democracy against Capitalism.* Cambridge: Cambridge University Press.

———. 1995b. "What Is the 'Postmodern' Agenda? An Introduction." *Monthly Review* 47: 1–12.

———. 1997. "Back to Marx." *Monthly Review* 49: 1–9.

Yudice, George. 1998. "The Globalization of Culture and the New Civil Society." In Sonia E. Alvarez, Evelina Dagnino, and Arturo Escobar, eds., *Cultures of Politics, Politics of Culture: Re-Visioning Latin American Social Movements.* Boulder, Colo.: Westview.

1

Flows, Networks, and Identities: A Critical Theory of the Informational Society

Manuel Castells

It is widely acknowledged that a process of structural transformation is under way in advanced societies. It stems from the combined impact of a major technological revolution based upon information–communication technologies, the formation of a global economy, and a process of cultural change whose main manifestations are the transformation of women's role in society and the rise of ecological consciousness. The recent transformation of the world political order and the demise of communism and of the Marxist–Leninist ideology are also fundamental trends of our historic epoch. Yet, I argue that the collapse of the Soviet empire is also a consequence of the strains generated by the transition to the informational society.

A number of social theories and interpretations have tried to grasp the essence of the current structural transformation (Beniger, 1986; Miles, 1988; Monk, 1989; Martin, 1988; Williams, 1988; Lyon, 1988; Katz, 1988; Salvaggio, 1989; Cawkell, 1987; Forester, 1987; Hage and Powers, 1992). They all agree on the centrality of knowledge generation and information processing as the basis of the new sociotechnical paradigm (Porat, 1977), as the technological–social revolution based on the generation and use of energy constituted the foundation of the industrial society (Kranzberg and Pursell, 1967). This is why I choose to name the new society "information-al," in order to indicate that the social attributes of information generation and information processing go beyond the impact of information technologies and of information itself, as the industrial society could not be simply assimilated to the diffusion of industrial manufacturing.

Yet, the brightness of the rising star often blinds the observer. Few theories are specific, comprehensive, and rigorous enough to provide an interpretive framework for the understanding of the new history. To be sure, there is a considerable amount of research on the social and economic impacts of new technologies, but these are partial aspects whose fundamental meaning has to be integrated into a broader system of social interaction. The systemic character of the theory is more necessary than ever to understand this new society, because one of the central features of such society is the tight interdependency between its social, political, and economic spheres.

There is also an abundance of pop sociological pseudotheories, confirming the fact that prophecies and ideologies quickly fill in the lack of scholarly research in any situation of historic transition. Overall, there is little systematic, rigorous theory enabling us to understand the actual contours of the social structure of contemporary societies as informational societies. Indeed, the best-constructed analyses of such process of transformation of the social structure are still based on the earlier, great sociological analyses of the postindustrial society. This is why we must return to the sources to build up from there, while contrasting the hypotheses on postindustrialism with the actual evolution of societies in the past twenty years.

Theories of the Postindustrial Society

It is a striking paradox that the theory of postindustrial society was formulated, in its essential nucleus, in the late 1960s (Touraine, 1969) and early 1970s (Bell, 1973), just before the full blossoming of the revolution in information technologies. Yet, today's social theorizing of structural transformation of our societies is still dominated by these early theoretical constructions, harbingers of a broader set of social and economic interpretations elaborated approximately in the same period (Richta, 1969; Fuchs, 1968; Porat, 1977). All these theories were based on the common idea that industrial society (not capitalism) has been historically superseded in its logic and structure. The fact that the theory anticipated the major technological transformations to come (the microprocessor, 1971; the personal computer, 1975; the recombination of DNA, 1973) shows that information technologies are an essential component of the overall social transformation, but it is not the only determinant factor. These technologies are the result of social and institutional demands for the tasks they can perform as well as the source of a series of fundamental transformations in the way we produce, consume, manage, live, and die.

In its essence, the theory of postindustrialism starts from a major empirical observation, that productivity and economic growth still organize societies around their logic, both in the work process and in the distribution of the wealth thus generated. In this sense, the theory is in line with the Marxian tradition. Furthermore, the engine for change to postindustrialism is an innovation in the productive forces; throughout the first half of the twentieth century, science and technology became the main sources of productivity. And in the post–World War II period, knowledge and information became the fundamental elements in the generation of wealth and power in society. This is the foundation of the theory. However, an immediate specification of such a statement makes things more complicated. Technology is not just science and machines; it is social and organizational technology, as well.

Indeed, in the first econometric analyses that founded the theory of postindustrialism (Solow, 1957; Kendrick, 1961) it was clear that the combination of production factors (basically labor and capital) and the efficient use of energy, all through organizational technology, were the basis for the hypotheses on the sources of productivity. According to these econometric analyses, the growth of productivity in industrialized economies did not come from the quantitative increase of capital or labor in the production process. It came from somewhere else, from a mysterious, unidentified, statistical residual that appeared in the equations characterizing the aggregate production function. It was hypothesized that such residual was the empirical expression of science, technology, and management.

Because both science (and its technological applications) and social technology (including, at some level, social science, along with managerial expertise) were considered to be the critical forces in the steady growth of productivity over time (above 2 percent per year in the United States), all social processes and institutions were to be involved in the productive forces. The various dimensions of society become more interdependent, and the worlds of economy and technology depend more than ever on government and, therefore, on the political process. Postindustrial societies, organized around social choices, are more political than agricultural societies (organized around survival against a hostile nature) and than industrial societies (organized around processes of economic accumulation).

Thus, the occupational structure of society becomes more diversified in terms of activity. The expansion of "services" means simply an ever-growing extension of human work beyond the sphere of direct, material production. Postindustrial societies are characterized, and even de-

fined in the thinking of some authors, by the shift from goods-produc-
ing to service-handling activities. This is the hard empirical trend
repeatedly used by social theorists as evidence of postindustrialism.
The decreasing weight of manufacturing in employment and in its contribution to gross domestic product is cited as the critical indicator for
the fading away of the industrial society.

Expansion of services is at the same time required and permitted by
the new productive forces. It is required because information processing, knowledge generation and distribution, and their supporting tasks
are critical for the generation of the economic surplus in an advanced,
information economy. But it is also the productivity generated in the
information economy that allows for the expansion of "service" activities, some of which (e.g., social services) are linked to the social demands of society rather than to the direct requests from the economy
(although they also have second-order effects in enhancing productivity). Thus, as a consequence of economic imperatives and of social–
institutional demands, a growing proportion of human activity and resources is devoted in our societies to information processing and other
non-goods-producing activities.

The transformation of the occupational structure is characterized by
the rise of highly educated social groups, in particular managers, professionals, and technicians. Among them, scientists and managers are
of foremost importance. From the perspective of postindustrial theory,
these groups are predicted to increase substantially in absolute number, in proportion to total employment, and in strategic importance in
organizations and society.

Social change is not limited to the transformation of social structure.
A new social structure is also linked to a new social dynamics, structurally opposing certain interests and creating new centers of conflict
and power making (the situses, in Bell's terminology). In this regard,
the theory offers two different, but not mutually exclusive, hypotheses:

1. The control over knowledge and information decides who holds
   power in society. Technocrats are the new dominant class, regardless of the fact that political power is exercised by politicians controlling the state. Who are the "dominated" classes? The answer
   of the theory on this point becomes more tenuous. In any case,
   they are not the workers, but the "citizens," the "consumers,"
   communities, the nonparticipant population. But they are also
   those professionals and experts who, while being part of the productivity establishment, are not part of its power system. As
   Alaine Touraine (1969) argues, it may be the professionals, lead-

ing the alienated citizens, who oppose the professionals and technocrats. The environmental movement is an example of the new social movements of the informational society (scientists and experts mobilizing consumers and citizens via the mass media on the basis of processing and communicating information about health, safety, and the conservation of nature).

2. The analysis of new social dynamics is easier if we define the structural logic behind the opposing interests. The dominant interests are those of scientific–technological rationality and economic growth. The alienated (rather than the dominated) interests are those of specific social identities. In Touraine's words, the fundamental opposition is between productivity and private life; or in Bell's words, between the meritocratic technical elites and the communal society. The mass media is the crucial instance of playing out the sociocultural battle, while the major social institutions expressing the orientations of society as a whole (education and health) are the privileged situses for the power games.

Theories of postindustrialism insist that the defining structural principle of the new society be placed on a different axis than the one opposing capitalism to statism. They deal with the technical relations of production not with the social (property-based) relations of production. The two axes should be considered in understanding any specific society.

In assessing the theory of postindustrial society more than twenty years after its initial, pathbreaking, formulation, several questions have to be dealt with in order to understand our societies and, thus, twenty-first-century societies:

1. Although all theories reject ethnocentrism and proclaim the diversity of national and cultural expressions of postindustrialism, their formulation in fact refers to the American and Western European experience (Daniel Bell basically ignores countries other than the United States and, in fact, assumes that America leads the way toward a future broadly common for all advanced societies). This is particularly embarrassing in the 1990s, when one of the most economically and technologically advanced societies, Japan, has to be taken into the picture, if the theory wants to be something other than an ad hoc description of the evolution of a given cultural context. This implies observing the evolution of Japan to see if and how it conforms to the theory. But more important, it involves the need to assess Japanese thinking on postin-

dustrialism in order to correct for the implicit ethnocentric bias of some American and European theories.

2. The relationship between manufacturing and services, the internal differentiation of service activities, and the specification of information processing and knowledge generation are questions still unsolved. The theory of postindustrialism points to the broad trends of the evolution but does not make critical differentiations inside the processes, nor does it establish the linkages among the sectors of activity under the new technological paradigm.

3. Although the theory has not been invalidated by the full blossoming and diffusion of the revolution in information technologies, the two decades of experience of such a revolution that we now have allow for a full reassessment of the original theoretical hypotheses in the light of the actual transformation of the technological paradigm. For instance, Bell's emphasis on "new intellectual technology" (simulation models and the like) has been much less relevant than he forecast, and the penetration of microelectronics and computer systems into the workplace have truly revolutionized work, organization, productivity, and competitiveness. Biology, not physics, is the decisive science of the twenty-first century. And universities do not seem to have emerged as the central institutions of the postindustrial society: corporations (both private and public), hospitals and health care systems, school systems, and the media are such central institutions, deeply transformed by the intensive use of new information and communication technologies.

4. Theories of postindustrialism generally overlook the specificity of women and the transformation of women's condition in advanced societies (with the exception of Bell's 1976 foreword to his 1973 publication regarding the expanded opportunities of employment for women in the postindustrial society). Yet, both the historical experience of these two decades and general theoretical reasons suggest that the specific analysis of women's roles and practices is not only a cornerstone of any social theory but also particularly relevant to the understanding of our societies.

5. A fundamental limit to the analysis of postindustrialism is that it refers to economic growth as the overarching value of our societies. It is not. Power, sheer power, has been all along as fundamental a goal as generation of wealth. Thus, the stimulation and appropriation of science and technology as a means of military power were as influential as the knowledge basis of productivity in the reshaping of our societies during and after World War II. In Bell's view, military technology is the new mode of production,

quite an ambiguous formulation. But such a fundamental remark is not fed back into the theory. Thus, it would seem that both economic productivity and state military power are at the source of overall social dynamics in our societies, and both (and their interaction) have been decisively affected by knowledge generation and technological innovation. A comprehensive theory of the informational society should break forever with the implicit economic view of postindustrialism.

6. On the other hand, postindustrial theory does not pay enough attention to a fundamental feature of our society. We live in an interdependent, global economy, whose internal linkages have been reinforced to the point of becoming inextricable, in a movement toward integration that accelerated as a way out of the 1973–74 world economic crisis. Societies are not reducible to economies, but it seems to be intellectually unacceptable that social structures could be analyzed independently of what happens at the level of the economic structure. This could be easily accepted by postindustrialist theories as far as it refers only to the North, namely the OECD countries (Bell, 1973, p. 483).

But what about the rest of the world? Bell does identify the problem but declares it to be "the outer limit of our trajectory—a problem for the twenty-first century" (p. 486). Touraine (1988) extensively, and probably more thoroughly than any one else, analyzes the contemporary dynamics of dependent societies. However, in both cases (a fortiori in other, less relevant, theoretical formulations of postindustrialism), the new social structure is analyzed as specific to the dominant, Western societies. With some rare exception (most notable, that of the work by Katz, 1988) less advanced societies are considered external to the system, and their effects on postindustrial societies are not taken into consideration, while the impacts of such new informational processes on the nonpostindustrial societies are not considered either. This approach reduces the explanatory power of any theory, not only because it leaves most of the planet out of its scope but also because it misses essential points of the dynamics of the most advanced societies.

Critical examples that justify my assertion are the following:

- The crisis and eventual demise of the Soviet empire cannot be understood without considering the internal contradictions generated in the Soviet economy and in the Soviet military machine by the logic of information-based technology and knowledge.

- The growing internal differentiation of the former Third World among newly industrializing countries (Asian Pacific), relatively self-sustaining societies (India, China), and decomposing societies (Sub-Saharan Africa) has much to do with the different degrees of integration and adaptation to the processes of the information economy.
- Immigration to OECD countries from the South is at the same time a consequence of the pattern of asymmetrical integration and a filling of the lower tier of the occupational structure of the information society.
- Drug production, drug trafficking, and drug consumption (a fundamental trend of our economies and societies) can be shown to be related both to the new infrastructure of communications and financial networks and to the sociocultural demands of the informational societies.

In sum, a theory of the information society that does not place the world's new economic interdependence at its heart is simply irrelevant for the purpose of understanding the new social structure of our societies. It is certainly easier to think of our societies as starting from their own internal logic, but such easy intellectual foundation misses a key point about our historical specificity. These are major issues to be addressed in shifting from the early theories of postindustrialism to a preliminary theorization of the informational society.

The Revolutionary Interaction of New Information Technologies with the Social System

Technological determinism is in essence the negation of social theory. Thus, we must reject from the onset any attempt at placing technological change at the roots of historical change. Yet, it is as important to acknowledge the extraordinary social change represented by new information technologies. In an obvious historical parallel, the steam engine did not create the industrial society by itself, but without the steam engine there would not have been an industrial society. Without the microprocessor and without the recombinant of DNA there would not be an informational society.

There is now general acceptance that in the last quarter of the twentieth century a technological revolution of historic proportions has taken shape (although, as always, the scientific foundations of such a revolution can be traced back much earlier, for instance to the 1912 discovery of the vacuum tube by De Forest at Stanford). Two basic features characterize the current technological revolution:

1. It is focused on process, as are all major technological revolutions, although it also spurs the continuous innovation of products. Because it is process oriented (as was the industrial revolution), its effects are pervasive and cut across all spheres of human activity.
2. Its fundamental raw material, as well as its principal outcome, is information, as the raw material of the industrial revolution was energy. In this, the information technology revolution is distinctive from preceding technological revolutions. While information and knowledge were always, by definition, essential elements in any process of scientific discovery and technical change, this is the first time in history in which the new knowledge applies primarily to the generation and processing of knowledge and information. Information technologies are not limited to microelectronics-based technologies. We must also include as a fundamental component of information technologies genetic engineering, since it deals with the decoding and eventual reprogramming of the codes of information contained in living matter. Indeed, the interaction between microelectronics-based information technologies and genetically based information technologies is the most fundamental frontier of science and technology in the twenty-first century.

How does this technology revolution affect society? To be sure, there is an interactive relationship between technology and society. Indeed, from the perspective of social theory, technology is a component, and an essential one, of society. The origins and trajectory of major technological changes are social. The application of technology is socially determined, as is the feedback on technology of the social consequences of its applications. Having granted all these crucial points, I think it is still important to focus upon the specific effects of this specific technological revolution on the social structure to understand the new, emerging social system.

The first distinctive feature is that, because information and knowledge are deeply embedded in the culture of societies, culture and symbol processing become direct productive forces in the new society. This blurs the traditional distinction between production and consumption and also supersedes the metaphysical debate about productive and unproductive labor. If symbol manipulation by a highly skilled, creative, and increasingly autonomous labor force becomes the fundamental source of productivity and competitiveness, all factors that contribute directly to the enhancement of such capacity are forces of production. The mental capacity of labor is certainly linked to education and training, but in an open, complex society, it depends as well on a variety of cultural and institutional conditions: health, communication, leisure, conditions of habitat, cultural recreation, travel, access to the natural environment, sociability, and so on. Thus, the processes of production and consumption, and beyond them the spheres of economic and social life, become increasingly intertwined.

A number of important institutional consequences follow from such observation. For instance, the welfare state cannot be seen simply as an unproductive, redistributive institution. By improving conditions of social life and cultural capacity, the welfare state, in its broadest sense, can be a decisive productive force in the informational society. The major distinction from the economic point of view is between types of welfare state institution, depending upon its role: enhancing social life for the majority of the population versus bureaucratic redistribution and stigma-prone charity. By ending the secular distinction between production and consumption in the social system, the new technological paradigm forces theory to analyze societies in terms of social relations, cutting across institutional spheres of social action.

A second major effect of new information technologies is that they link processes of production, distribution, and management across organizations and across types of activity. Thus, manufacturing or agriculture cannot be conceived independently of the information and service activities embedded into the production of goods. And the employment and occupational structure cannot be considered to follow the linear, historical succession from primary to secondary sectors and then to tertiary activities. Instead, there is a fundamental change from a techno-organizational division of labor to a complex matrix of linkages of productive and management activities that command the logic of the entire occupational system.

To test this analysis, I studied, with my assistant Yuko Aoyama, the evolution of the employment and occupational structure of the G-7 countries between 1920 and 2005 (Castells and Aoyama, 1993). The findings unveil some surprises for the postindustrialist dogma. Japan and Germany, while having become the most competitive and technologically advanced economies, display a much higher level of manufacturing employment than the United States or the United Kingdom and a much lower level of information workforce. It does not follow, however, that information is not important in Japan. What appears to happen is that the linkage between information processing and material production takes different organizational forms in different institutional and managerial structures (e.g., Japanese and German manufacturing firms internalize a higher proportion of their own services; also, a much lower proportion of Japan's and Germany's industrial production is done offshore).

In sum, information technologies allow different types of activity to link up according to the organizational form that suits the strategy of the firm or the history of the institution. The flexibility of new technologies allows for a diversity of organizational arrangements, which make it possible for people to work together in different firms, in different locations, in different sectors of activity. It follows that the traditional distinction between agriculture and services and between manufacturing and services, as well as the enormous diversity of "service activities," does not make sense any more.

Furthermore, new information technologies allow for the constitution of a production and management system spread all over the world yet working on real time and working as a unit through the combination of telecommunications, fast transportation, and computerized flexible production systems. This worldwide production system does not concern only the multinational corporations. Networks of firms, and the ancillary networks of suppliers and distributors, also gravitate around global production and management flows (Castells, 1989). The process is most obvious in the case of the global financial markets (Sassen, 1991). Three critical concepts emerge from such fundamental transformation in the way the new production system operates: linkages between activities, networks made up of organizations, and flows of production factors and of commodities. Together, they form the basis of the new economy and will force the redefinition of the occupational structure and, thus, of the class system of the new society.

The same logic applies to the fundamental process of organizational change under way, a third major distinctive effect of information technologies. As complexity and uncertainty become essential characteristics of the new environment in which organizations must operate, the fundamental needs for the management of organizations are those of flexibility and adaptability (Benveniste, forthcoming): flexibility to gear the external system of the organization toward the requests of a rapidly changing world, adaptability to modify the internal system of the organization in accordance with each new pattern of strategic guidance. The demands for such organizational changes have existed for some time in the marketplace. But it was only with the spread of affordable information technologies that firms and institutions were able to decentralize and become flexible without undermining their control and guidance systems. Thus, small and medium firms were able to link up, relate to a broader market, and become suppliers to large firms, adding substantial flexibility to the system. Multinational corporations decentralized their units to the point of forming constellations of quasi-independent entities.

Major firms formed strategic alliances, joint ventures, and partnerships in different product lines and in different markets and functions, often becoming competitors of their own allies in specific areas. While the concentration of wealth and power in major conglomerates has continued in most countries and at the world level, the structure of the economy and of social institutions has become increasingly decentralized and diversified, with a growing number of units making their own decisions, while relating to a complex system of hierarchies, alliances, and competitions. Overall, and as a general trend, multidirectional networks are substituting for vertical bureaucracies as the most efficient, archetypical form of the new system, on the basis of flexible, affordable, and increasingly powerful information and communication technologies.

The direct impact on the media—and thus on the formation of images, representations, and public opinion in our societies—is a direct, obvious impact of new communication technologies. This has been the object of endless studies and interpretations, to the point that it seems hardly necessary to further elaborate on the issue. And yet, new communication technologies have made obsolete the "classic" television era, forcing us to reconsider the new interaction between communication and communication technologies. What is new in the new media, as they have been affected by satellite transmission, cable, VCRs, portable communication devices, and eventually microwave transmission, is the simultaneous tendency toward globalization and individualization of image making, sound making, and broadcasting.

On the one hand, the whole planet is (unevenly) connected in global networks of the information and images that travel throughout the world instantly. On the other hand, the media are less and less mass oriented. Markets and audiences (ultimately the same) have been segmented and specifically targeted. The emergence of specialized networks, through cable television or satellite transmission, depending on the society, is not only a challenge to traditional TV networks, it is a new form of image distribution and reception. Together with specialized radio stations, they are forming a new media system that looks for specific audiences or specific moods and tastes of general audiences. VCRs are also becoming powerful instruments of individualization, since they are decreasingly used to view rented films and increasingly used for videotaping films and events, thus selecting available images while preserving the time and conditions of image consumption. The Walkman device (that will shortly have its video equivalent, beyond the current primitive wrist TV sets) reaches the ultimate individualization for the reception of messages, moving from mass media to individual consumption and to the segmented distribution of a flexible, global production of audiovisual messages. To some extent, now, the message is the medium, since it is the message that determines the medium to be used as well as the how, where, when, and for whom.

In a related development, the rapid diffusion of virtual reality representation in computer networks creates the possibility of individualized, self-programmable, image representation and perception, which will increasingly disconnect individuals from the mass media, while connecting the individualized communication expressions to the individuals' mental world. The social consequence of such technological developments is the growing tension between globalization and individualization in the audiovisual universe, bringing about the danger of a breakdown in the patterns of social communication between world information flows and personal experiences.

Last but not least, the strategic character of information technologies in the productivity of the economy and in the efficacy of social institutions changes the sources of power within society and among societies. The mastery of the science and technology of information technologies becomes a source of power in itself. Granted, the state, because it still holds the institutional monopoly of violence, remains the source of power in society. But a state incapable of keeping up with the rapid, endless process of technological change will become a weak state both internally (its economic basis will deteriorate) and externally (the coercive means of its institutional monopoly of violence will become technologically obsolete). This is a fundamental development, because the ability to foster technological change under the new conditions of information technology revolution are directly related to the ability of a society to diffuse and exchange information and to relate to the rest of the world.

On both counts, military and secluded empires cannot compete with open societies and market economies in the fostering of new technologies. Nuclear power is in fact the last, most destructive, technology of the industrial era. Communication technologies can indeed be used for purposes of military destruction and police control, but the potential of an institutional system to develop communication technologies depends on a number of social conditions that found serious obstacles in closed societies and military-oriented apparatuses (Guile, 1985). The surprising collapse of the Soviet empire is the most striking evidence supporting this hypothesis. The inability of the Soviet system to compete with the West in information technologies decisively undermined its military power, opening the way for a last-ditch attempt at reforming the system—which eventually precipitated its demise (for a tentative analysis of this process, see Castells, 1992).

The Transformation of Women's Condition and the Social Redefinition of Family, Sexuality, and Personality

A fundamental feature of the new society is the transformation of women's condition in the most developed countries. At the roots of such transformation, which has taken place at an accelerated pace since the 1960s, are two interrelated phenomena: the massive entry of women into the labor market in most advanced economies and the social movements based on the defense of identity that nurtured the development of the women's movement and of feminism in general. Both structural change and social mobilization are important to understand the transformation of women's roles and values in society. But because feminist and women's movements had already taken place in earlier historical periods, I am inclined to attribute the greatest weight in the process of change to the transformation of the labor market and the subsequent access of women to paid jobs, even though under conditions of structural discrimination. Thus, the transformation of the employment structure under the conditions of the rising information economy is directly related to the change in women's position in society.

Whatever the causes, women engaging in a lifelong perspective as workers found themselves in a better bargaining position at home, while the social division of labor between the breadwinner and the homemaker lost its basis of cultural legitimation. At the same time, having to cope simultaneously with four tasks (working for pay, keeping the house, rearing the children, and managing the husband) stressed women's everyday life to the limit in a context in which society was not matching the incorporation of women into the workforce with the provision of services for the functioning of the household. There followed among women a great deal of receptivity for the feminist values debated in the media at the initiative of social movements and ideologists. Thus, while most women in most societies would not call themselves feminists, a dramatic change in the values of society, and particularly in the values of women, took place in just one generation. Equal rights became an institutional goal for most women. But more important, the overwhelming majority of women of advanced countries in the 1990s do not accept the values underlying the social institution of the patriarchal family. Gender discrimination is still a fact in all societies, and the true sharing of housework is still negligible in the population at large. But the structure of legitimation of patriarchalism has been fundamentally shaken. Women do not accept men's authority any more. The power game has to be played out now on an interpersonal basis—the institutions of society cannot come to the rescue of patriarchalism. The penetration of women's demands in the media and the rapid political mobilization of women have made substantial inroads in the structure of power of all societies, signaling unmistakably the historical trend toward gender equality.

Granted, thousands of years of patriarchalism will not disappear easily. The ingrained reflexes of gender domination will remain alive for generations, transmitted by some of the most fundamental cultural values of society. Yet, the economic need to incorporate women into the labor force, the political interest in appealing to women voters, and the pressures of a powerful, if diffused and divided, feminist movement combine to create a new historical ground that has already had a fundamental impact on the overall social system.

The first and most important impact has been on the family. The patriarchal family has been called into question, and a period of institutional crisis has followed, as in all historical transitions. Women's demands in their partnerships find strong resistance from men, who see their interests threatened and their values called into question. Separatism between genders has been on the rise, with the divorce rate rising in most societies and the number of single households exploding. In the United States, for instance, more than 50 percent of marriages end in a divorce. Also, the traditional family, formed by a married couple with children, is today the exception in the United States: only 25 percent of households fit that model. Single-parent families are the fastest-growing category, followed by singles, then by couples without children. Although patriarchal nuclear families resist the trend better in Western Europe (and still thrive in Japan), the trends toward the disintegration of such model are similar in all societies. For couples who stay together, there has been a fundamental transformation of family roles. Dual-career households have become the norm, and constant negotiations are needed to accommodate each member's professional life.

Because society continues to consider providing child care for the whole working population a nonnecessary service, the caring for children has become a fundamental element around which family life revolves. Different societies adapt differently to the child care crisis. In Western Europe extended family relationships cushion the crisis, with grandparents doing a share of family work—which interestingly leads to the revitalization of extended family relationships. In the United States, in what I would expect to be the general norm as other societies reach the same high rate of women's participation in the labor force, two main avenues are taken to care for children, depending on social class. For the professional middle class, women subcontract their child care to domestic workers, mainly from Third World countries. For working-class women, they rely on support networks that socialize child care on the basis of the neighborhood. In both cases, the patterns of socialization of children are fundamentally affected. In addition, while men continue to participate very little in domestic work, they do take more care of the children, because of the emotional rewards involved. The net result is that the new generations are being socialized out of the traditional pattern of the patriarchal family and being exposed from an early age to the need to cope with different worlds and different adult roles. In sociological terms, the new process of socialization downplays to some extent the role of the patriarchal family and diversifies the roles within the family world. As a result, we would expect to see more complex personalities, less secure yet more capable of adapting to changing roles and social contexts (see Hage and Powers, 1992, on this subject).

The increasing individualization of relationships within the family tends to emphasize the importance of personal demands beyond the rules of the institution. Thus, to some extent sexuality becomes, at the level of social values, a personal need that does not necessary have to be channeled and institutionalized within the family. With the majority of the adult population living outside the boundaries of the traditional nuclear family, the expression of sexuality concentrates on interpersonal relationships and becomes an open dimension of the new self. The socialization of teenagers in such new cultural patterns leads to a dramatically higher degree of sexual freedom in comparison to that of preceding generations. This is why even the threat of contracting AIDS has not reduced promiscuity among teenagers.

The open expression of sexuality and the slow but growing acceptance of sexuality by society have allowed the expression of homosexuality, fostered by powerful gay and lesbian movements that have become major agents of cultural change. Indeed, the gay movement, at least according to the findings of my study on San Francisco's gay community, is not only a movement for the defense of gay rights but also a movement for the legitimation of sexuality in society, without boundaries or controls relative to kind of sexuality.

Thus, the revolt of women against their condition at home, induced and allowed by their massive entry into the information labor force, has called into question the partriarchal nuclear family. The crisis of the traditional family has increased the separation between the dimensions previously held together by that institution:

- Interpersonal relationships between the two members of the couple.
- The professional life of each member of the household.
- The economic association of the members of the household.
- The distribution of domestic work.
- The raising of the children.
- Sexuality.

The difficulty in coping with all these dimensions, once they are not fixed in formal structure such as the patriarchal family, explains the difficulty in maintaining stable social relationships within the family-based household. It is obvious that for families to survive, new institutionalized forms of social relationships, in accordance with the new social roles and functions of women, will have to emerge.

At the same time, technological change in reproductive techniques has allowed the possibility of dissociating the reproduction function from the social and personal functions of the family. The possibilities of in-vitro fertilization, of surrogate mothers, and of laboratory-produced babies open up a whole new area of social experimentation, which society will try to control and repress as much as possible because of its potential threat to our moral and legal foundations. Yet, that women can have children on their own without having to even know the father and that men can use surrogate mothers to have their children break down the fundamental relationship between biology and society in the reproduction of the human species, thus separating socialization from parenting. Under such historical conditions, families are being redefined in terms that are still unclear.

Because family and sexuality are fundamental determinants of personality systems, the calling into question of known family structures and the coming into the open of sexuality bring about the possibility of new types of personality that we are just starting to perceive. My hypothesis combines Jerald Hage and Charles Powers' views (1992) with a more adventurous speculation. I agree with them that the key ability to respond to current changes in society at the individual level is the ability to engage in "role redefinition," what they consider to be the "pivotal micro-process" of postindustrial society. While this is a fundamental statement, it is too general: it does not allow us to specify the social dynamics emerging in the new historical context. Let us try a complementary approach to their analysis of new, emerging personality systems.

If we dare to introduce some elements of psychoanalytical theory in this excursus, we could say that the open recognition of individual desire would lead to such an aberration as the institutionalization of desire. Because desire, is, by definition, constant transgression, the recognition of sexuality outside the family would lead to extreme social stress. As long as the transgression consists merely in expressing sexuality outside the family boundaries, society could easily cope with it, channeling it through coded situations and organized contexts (e.g., prostitution, tolerated sexual harassment, etc.). But the patriarchal family is not there any more to be betrayed, the transgression will have to become an individual act against society. The bumper function of the family is lost, which opens the way to the expression of desire in the form of irrational violence. The breaking down of the traditional family (the only one existing until now) is indeed giving way to the normalization of sexuality (pornographic movies during prime-time television broadcasting) and to the spread of senseless violence in society through the back alleys of uncontrolled desire.

The liberation of the family confronts the self with its own inflicted oppression. The escape to freedom in the open, informational society will lead to individual anxiety and social violence until new forms of control are found that bring together men, women, and children in a reconstructed family structure better suited to the taming of liberated women and uncertain men.

The Global Economy, the Informational Society, and the Interdependence of Social Structure across the World

We live in a global economy. This is not the same as a world economy, a reality that has existed since the sixteenth century. A global economy is an economy in which all processes work as a unit on real time throughout the planet; that is, an economy in which capital flows, labor markets, markets, the production process, management, information, and technology operate simultaneously at the world level. This is not to say that nations and nation-states disappear. In fact, states become major players in the global economy on the basis of the defense of the specific national interests they represent. But the economic unit of operation (and of analysis) is the global system of interactions. There are no more national economies and national economic policies; they are nationally based strategies operating in a global system differentiated and articulated across and between national boundaries. In a book on the global economy in the information age, which I wrote with Martin Carnoy, Stephen Cohen, and Fernando Henrique Cardoso (Carnoy et al., 1993), we show the close connection between the globalization and informationalization of the economy and try to analyze the structure and dynamics of the new global economy. Thus, I will not elaborate further on the economic dimension of my analysis. What I want to emphasize here is the consequence of such analysis for the theory of the informational society.

If the economies across the planet are linked, how can societies be analyzed independently? Unless we assert that economies and societies are entirely autonomous systems, if there is a global economy, there must be a structural relationship among the societies integrated into such an economy. Thus, the theory of the informational society cannot concentrate exclusively on the most advanced societies. It must also account for the structure of dependent societies and for the interactive effects between social structures asymmetrically located along the networks of the global economy.

To be sure, information technologies have spread across the whole world, and the information workforce has increased in all countries. However, the study by Raul Katz (1988), the only existing study on the informational society from a truly international perspective, shows that the meaning of the information workforce in "developing" countries is very different from that in advanced countries. Its expansion is mainly linked to government employment and is concentrated on generally unproductive activities. Also, he shows a limited diffusion of information technologies in most of these countries, and that is generally under government supervision. Evaluation of the role of information technology industries in Third World development shows the gigantic gap between most countries on this planet and the OECD area. On the other hand, the ability of the newly industrializing countries to adapt, produce, and diffuse new information technologies has become the critical factor for their development.

Thus, there is not a necessary, single path that all countries must follow toward the informational society. But there is a comprehensive global structure based on the rules of the informational society that affects all countries in one way or the other. First, the ability to use (and to some extent to produce) information technologies has become a fundamental tool of development. It is the historical equivalent to electrification in earlier stages of development. But we know that the use of information technologies is not only a matter of hardware. Without the information capacity of society, that is without information labor, organizations, and institutions, there will be little chance for developing countries to develop. Technological dependency, in the broadest sense of the notion, becomes the fundamental obstacle for development in our world.

Second, the whole world becomes interconnected in its economic functions through information and communication flows. Access to such flows becomes critical for any economy and, thus, for any society.

Being switched off the network is the equivalent of not existing in the global economy. The position in the network—that is, the function obtained in the new international division of labor—becomes an essential element in defining each country's or region's material conditions of existence.

Third, the information economy, while connecting the whole planet in a series of networks of flows, does so selectively. Because productivity and competitiveness rely less and less on primary resources and more and more on knowledge and information, cheap, unskilled labor and raw materials cease to be strategic inputs in the new economy. Large areas of the world are increasingly irrelevant for the global information economy. The exploitation of labor or natural resources becomes too costly for the benefit obtained. As the economy evolves toward higher value-added, information-based products, the accumulation of capital proceeds at the core, not at the periphery. The economic theories of imperialism are now doomed. In the new economy, markets, skilled labor, capital, and technology are increasingly concentrated in the OECD countries, with the addition of a few newly industrializing economies and the fundamental addition of China as a potential economic superpower. Beyond that, the incorporation of Eastern Europe and Russia into the core system will provide markets and the required natural resources (drawn from Siberia) for the system to thrive for a long time.

The consequence is that many countries, and many regions of many countries, are being bypassed by the expansion of the global information economy. National, local, and regional societies are shifting from a position of dependent exploitation to structural irrelevance in the new economy. Such development is triggering several processes, all part of the new social structure characteristic of the informational society:

- The increasing dualization of dependent societies, with a few segments incorporated into the global economy and culture, and with marginality spreading in a variable but substantial proportion of the population.
- A desperate attempt by excluded societies to reject the rules of the game by affirming their cultural identity in fundamentalist terms, opening the way for a variety of *jihads* against the infidels of the dominant order.
- Efforts by marginalized countries to establish what I call "the perverse connection" to the global economy, specializing in criminal trade: drugs, weapons, money laundering, traffic of human beings (women to prostitute, babies to adopt, human organs to be transplanted, etc.).

- Reconstructing the unity of the world by mass migrations to the core countries in flows of people that could only be stopped by massive police measures that would fundamentally affect the character of democracy in advanced countries.

The separation between the dynamic of the global economy and the structure of the informational society is transforming the social fabric of both advanced and dependent countries in a fundamental way. The reintegration of both processes in an articulated historical practice requires a concerted body of institutional action, which does not exist today.

The process of historical transition to the information economy is likely to be dominated by the fundamental disjunction between, on the one hand, a global economy and a worldwide information network and, on the other hand, nationalistic civil societies, communal cultures, and increasingly parochial states.

The Society of Flows

After twenty years of efforts to describe, analyze, and theorize the "new society," there is still a great deal of uncertainty about what this society is. The reconstruction of a theoretical paradigm suitable to the new social processes we are observing must start from a critical observation that should have become apparent in the preceding pages of this chapter. Our societies are fundamentally made of flows exchanged through networks of organizations and institutions. By *flows* I mean purposeful, repetitive, programmable sequences of exchange and interaction between physically disjointed positions held by social actors in organizations and institutions of society. The convergence of social evolution and information technologies has created a new material basis for the performance of the activities processed through the social system. This material basis is so historically specific that it imposes its inherent logic on most social processes, thus essentially conditioning the structure of society.

The determination of these networks of flows over the social structure operates at least at four levels:

1. Networks organize the positions of actors, organizations, and institutions in societies and economies. Social relevance of any social unit is thus conditioned by its presence or absence in specific networks. The absence of a dominant network leads to structural irrelevance. Only life in the networks amounts to social existence,

in accordance with the structurally dominant values and interests. Because networks shape in an uneven way societies, segments of society, social groups, and individuals, the most fundamental social distinction refers to the position in a given network. Examples of such logic are the positions of countries or regions in the world economy (some areas being structurally irrelevant and including their populations in their irrelevance; other areas being nodal) and the position of individuals of different educational levels in the new organizational structure (information holders and generators of knowledge are critical to the organization, while information-processing executants are periodically displaced by automation).

2. There are also important differences within networks and between networks in terms of the structural importance of the flows generated in such networks (or in some network's position) for a given system's goals. The structural hierarchy between networks and between positions within a network's flows largely determines the ability to influence the overall social logic from a particular position. However, such hierarchy is unstable and may constantly change, depending on the transformation of social conditions. The critical question concerning the dynamic of society is that of the relationship between the change in the hierarchy of flows and the changes in the allocation of individuals to the positions in these flows. For instance, a region may increase or decrease its competitiveness in the world economy, thus reflecting these changes in the economic conditions of its residents. But it is crucial to know whether, when there is decline, the region's residents suffer a decline in their position in the economic networks although, when there is prosperity, a labor force of outsiders is brought in because they fit better the requirements of the worldwide networks for the region's revival.

3. Within networks, there are important asymmetries between positions. CEOs of major financial institutions have a dominant position vis-à-vis borrowers; reviewers of scientific journals control the innovation efforts of young researchers; news editors of television networks shape the content of information for the viewers; factory floor managers organize the teamwork that leads to specific production procedures, and so on. Who sends the message and who shapes the channel of transmission of the flow largely condition the social effects of communication flows, be it an order, an investment, an instruction, or a self-serving image.

Yet, the networks of flows tend to become largely independent of the power holders controlling the nodes of the network. The flows of power are easily transformed into the power of flows. This is a fundamental characteristic of the new society. An obvious example is that of financial markets: once a speculative movement is triggered in the international market, the reserves of the central banks of the wealthiest nations may be gobbled up in a few days while trying to go against the flow. Who are these speculators? Many people and nobody. There are certainly organizations (actually network) living off the turmoil in the financial markets, but they have no real power by themselves. Their role is to trigger a dynamic of flows that surpasses by far any organization's (or group of organizations) wealth and power. In some cases, the computers themselves, by the random effect of their programs being triggered at the same time in preventive buying or selling, are the "speculators." Similar, although less powerful, examples may be found in the world of political images, of intellectual fashion, and of commercial music. In all cases, extremely important social, economic, and cultural consequences follow the formation of turbulences in the space of flows. I am not arguing that social action becomes random. I am arguing that a structural logic dominated by largely uncontrollable flows within and between networks creates the conditions for the unpredictability of the consequences of human action through the reflection of such action in an unseen, uncharted space of flows.

4. The logic of flows in our societies is universal but not comprehensive. Selective networks cover through their flows all spheres of society and all areas of the planet. But they segment countries and people according to the specific goals of each network and the specific characteristics of people and countries. It follows an extremely uneven social geography, in which the structural meaning for each locale, for each group, for each person is deconstructed from its experience and reconstructed in the flows of the network. The reaction against such destructuration takes the form of affirming basic cultural, historical, or biological identities (real or reconstructed) as fundamental principles of existence. The society of flows is also a society of primary ascription communities, in which the affirmation of the being (ethnic identity, territorial identity, gender identity, religious identity, historic identity, national identity) becomes the organizing principle for a system that in itself becomes a system for itself.

Under such conditions, we could predict a tendency toward the breakdown of the communication pattern between the dominant institutions of society, working along ahistorical, abstract networks of functional flows, and the dominated communities, defending their existence around the principle of irreducible, fundamental, noncommunicable identity. A society made up of the juxtaposition of flows and tribes ceases to be a society. The structural logic of the information age bears the seeds of a new, fundamental barbarianism.

The structural domination of the organizational logic of networks and of the relational logic of flows has substantial consequences for the social structure, consequences that are often considered as indicators of the new informational society. In fact, they are the manifestation of a deeper trend: the emergence of flows as the stuff from which our societies are made. I hypothesize below the main consequences of such a fundamental historical trend:

- The ability to generate new knowledge and to gather strategic information depends on access to the flows of such knowledge or information, be it flows between major research centers or insider knowledge in Wall Street trading. It follows that the power of organizations and the fortune of individuals depend on their positioning vis-à-vis such sources of knowledge and on their capacity to understand and process such knowledge. It is in this fundamental sense that we live in a knowledge-based, informational society. But the key point to keep in mind is that there is no single, privileged source of science or information. Knowledge is also a flow. No researcher, or research center, can survive in isolation in modern science. No financial investment can be made without specialized information about the market—that is, about the flow of transactions.

- The productivity and competitiveness of the economic system, a fundamental subsystem in our society, depend on the position of economic units in the networks of the global economy. These units may be firms, cities, regions, countries, or economic areas (such as the EEC). They all depend on their positioning in a network of economic exchanges. Such a network is not only the market. It is a market submitted to government intervention, to technological change, to business's privileged information, to firms' strategies, and to worldwide flows of capital, labor, and raw materials. So the actual operational network is made up of a networking of networks, making the structure of flows so complex that the successful positioning ultimately depends on an advantageous relationship of the economic unit to a flow that happens to be strategic: for example, Silicon Valley firms' historical relationship to Stanford University; Japanese firms' luck of being national champions for MITI's nationalist project; Airbus's connection to the last stand of French grandeur. Thus, economic dominance ultimately depends on the relative position vis-à-vis a flow in the overall system of networks. Relative positions can indeed be changed, and this is what competition is all about. But such changes also depend on the ability to maneuver economic flows through flows of information (better management, better marketing strategy, more educated labor, better access to suppliers' networks, better technology, etc.).

- The flows of images/sounds/messages created by the new media are fundamental elements in shaping the representation and communication patterns of our societies. We left the Gutenberg galaxy some time ago, and we live now, as I briefly mentioned above, in a collection of related constellations, made up of specialized audiovisual universes living off the bridges formed by worldwide networks of information and entertainment.

- The political system is now fundamentally dependent upon the skilled manipulation of messages and symbols. The media are the fundamental battleground for political control, at least in the democratic systems. Reality is increasingly mediated by the media, because they are indeed the virtual reality of the majority of the population. A good example of the absolute intertwining between media and politics was the incident in the 1992 American presidential campaign when Vice President Dan Quayle criticized a television character ("Murphy Brown") for having a child out of wedlock—to which "Murphy Brown" responded in a heated argument in a subsequent episode of the series, thus engaging a crucial political debate about morality between a television character and the vice president of the United States. Of course, the television character won the debate, as history will record.

  Politics that does not exist in the media, particularly in television, simply does not exist in today's democratic politics. To the extent that other forms of political expression are relevant, they are also based on networks of a different kind: local networks or organizational networks, linked to a strong, historically rooted, political basis, such as local chapters of a party or labor union organizations under direct party influence. Indeed, the only political parties that still have a relevant function as parties, different from mere electoral machines, are those with widespread grassroots organizations that provide an adequate ground for a targeted deployment of a media-oriented political strategy (e.g., cheering, crowded political rallies have as their major function the portrayal of the image of popular support for the candidate's personality and ideas).

The personalization of politics is a fundamental trend in all societies. Because the candidates are symbols, their personalities are scrutinized in the media, and the result of such scrutiny is often decisive for their political fate. Thus, flows of images and information are the critical ingredients of political power. Power does not lie any more along the barrel of a gun but lies, instead, in the editing programs of the television networks' computers.

- Because the materiality of our existence is made up of flows or of community-based resistance to such flows, representation of values and interests are not structured any more on the basis of work. They are expressed either in terms of a symbolic message or in terms of the defense of primary identities of self-identified communities. Thus, collective action is often expressed as a rejection to the logic of flows on behalf of ethnic communities, local communities, gender communities, or culturally and biologically defined communities (the handicapped, gays, etc.). Sometimes, the rejection is addressed against other communities, similarly identified in terms of primary ascription. This is frequently the basis for racism and xenophobia.

- Collective action that breaks through ascribed social conditions is constructed around messages and symbols that strike the chord of a diverse, unpredictable constituency, from an indignant reaction against political corruption to the defense of whales. These messages are usually generated, or at least transmitted, in the world of the media, therefore in a world of flows of images and representations. Their appeal often cuts across a broad segment of the population, although it generally mobilizes more easily the better educated groups. This symbol-triggered mobilization can be the result of deliberate action, as is often the case with the environmental movement. But more often than not its success depends on random circumstances. If my hypothesis is correct, then we have lost the direct linkage between the structure of social organization in terms of identifiable material interests and the logic of social mobilization. Processes of change occur according to a symbolic logic located in the processes of representation of the space of flows.

- Such tendencies lead to the demise of forms of collective action that are neither rooted in primary identities nor triggered by a powerful symbol. This is for instance the case of the labor movement, which has become a professionalized organization specializing in articulating and negotiating grievances of various interest groups. Thus, when the Berkeley teaching assistants went on strike in 1992 asking the right to be represented in their teaching conditions by the United Auto Workers Union, they were in fact demonstrating the demise of the labor movement they wanted to bolster. If the UAW can represent Berkeley graduate students, it means that the linkage between position in the social structure and representation of interests has been lost, to the benefit of professionalized representatives mastering the technology of litigation and bargaining.

- At the level of personal interaction, Hage and Powers (1992) brilliantly hypothesize that what characterizes the new society is the endless construction of the self by people engaging in the interaction process, instead of representing themselves in everyday life à la Goffman. This is because the constant changes in roles and situations in a society defined by innovation, flexibility, and unpredictability in all spheres require people to constantly redefine themselves in their roles at work, in the family, and with their friends. Therefore, the restructuring of the personality to adequately fulfill the new functions demanded by society requires a bringing together of all the new codes and messages from the different networks relating to the various dimensions of people's lives. The construction and reconstruction of the self is tantamount to manage the changing set of flows and codes that people are confronted with in their daily experience.

Thus, the materiality of networks and flows does create a new social structure at all levels of society. It is this social structure that actually constitutes the new informational society, a society that could be more properly named the society of flows, since flows are made up not only of information but also of all materials of human activity (capital, labor, commodities, images, travelers, changing roles in personal interaction, etc.).

References

Bell, Daniel. 1973. *The Coming of Post-Industrial Society: A Venture in Social Forecasting*. New York: Basic Books.

Beniger, James R. 1986. *The Control Revolution: Technological and Economic Origins of the Information Society*. Cambridge: Harvard University Press.

Benveniste, Guy. Forthcoming. *Twenty-first Century Organizations*. San Francisco: Jossey-Bass.

Carnoy, Martin, et al. 1993. *The New Global Economy in the Information Age*. University Park: Penn State University Press.

Castells, Manuel. 1989. *The Informational City*. Oxford: Basil Blackwell.

———. 1992. *La Nueva Revolucion Rusa*. Madrid: Sistema.

Castells, Manuel, and Yuko Aoyama. 1993. "Paths toward the Informational

Society: The Transformation of the Employment Structure of G-7 Countries, 1920–2005." BRIE Working Paper. University of California, Berkeley, Institute of International Studies.

Cawkell, A. E., ed. 1987. *Evolution of an Information Society*. London: Aslib.

Forester, Tom. 1987. *High Tech Society: The Story of the Information Technology Revolution*. Oxford: Basil Blackwell.

Fuchs, Victor. 1968. *The Service Economy*. New York: National Bureau of Economic Research.

Guile, Bruce, comp. 1985. *Information Technology and Social Transformation*. Washington, D.C.: National Academy Press.

Hage, Jerald, and Charles Powers. 1992. *Post-Industrial Lives: Roles and Relationships in the 21st Century*. London: Sage.

Katz, Raul Luciano. 1988. *The Information Society: An International Perspective*. New York: Praeger.

Kendrick, John. 1961. *Productivity Trends in the United States*. Princeton: Princeton University Press.

Kranzberg, Melvin, and Carroll W. Pursell, eds. 1967. *Technology in Western Civilization*. New York: Oxford University Press.

Lyon, David. 1988. *The Information Society: Issues and Illusions*. Cambridge: Polity.

Martin, William. 1988. *The Information Society*. London: Aslib.

Miles, Ian, et al. 1988. *Information Horizons: The Long-Term Implications of New Information Technologies*. Hants: E. Elgar.

Monk, Peter. 1989. *Technological Change in the Information Economy*. London: Pinter.

Porat, Marc. 1977. *The Information Economy*. Washington, D.C.: Department of Commerce, Office of Telecommunications.

Richta, Radovan. 1969. *La Civilisation au Carrefour*. Paris: Anthropos.

Salvaggio, Jerry L., ed. 1989. *The Information Society: Economic, Social, and Structural Issues*. Hillsdale, N.J.: Erlbaum.

Sassen, Saskia. 1991. *Global Cities*. Princeton: Princeton University Press.

Solow, Robert M. 1957. "Technical Change and the Aggregate Production Function." *Review of Economics and Statistics* 39 (August).

Touraine, Alain. 1969. *La Societe Post-Industrielle*. Paris: Denoel.

———. 1988. *La Parole et le Sang. Politique et Societe en Amerique Latine*. Paris: Odile Jacob.

Williams, Frederick, ed. 1988. *Measuring the Information Society*. Beverly Hills: Sage.

2

New Educational Inequalities

Ramón Flecha

The Dual Model of the Information Society

We are already far advanced in the emergence of a new type of society, which is generating new forms of inequality. Since industrial society entered into crisis, this new situation has been labeled postindustrial society and defined essentially by those aspects of it that are no longer the same as before.[1] However, this concept is as unilluminating on the eve of the twenty-first century as it would have been to describe the situation in the nineteenth century as postfeudal and try to explain it in terms of what was no longer the same as in the fifteenth century.

The identification of the causes of the crisis and the attempts to resolve it, which have taken place in the last years, have made possible important advances in the analysis of the new reality. We are therefore in a position to characterize the current information society not simply in terms of what is no longer the same but in terms of what is new. These advances allow us to design projects for the future and, therefore, to intervene in its transformation. In our analysis of new educational inequalities, we can identify three general characteristics of the dual model of the information society: intellectual resources, social dualization, and a dissolution of solidarity.

From Material to Intellectual Resources

The impact of the new information revolution is being felt in more and more areas of human life. Information processing is becoming one of the determining factors in the economy and in all areas of our social life, from the growing importance of design (information added to a product) to a relative increase in the importance of families' cultural rather than economic capital in determining educational performance.

This situation means that mental capacities are much more decisive than they were in the industrial society. Increasingly, success in different areas of social life depends on the culture we carry with us, the knowledge and skills we possess. This has led some to claim that the information society is more democratic and egalitarian than its predecessors because material resources, which predominate in industrial society, are extremely unequally distributed, while mental factors, which now predominate, are given to all.

Social Dualization

Although the information revolution creates opportunities for improving the conditions of human existence, the social model that is becoming hegemonic in its wake deepens existing inequalities and generates others. One of the most important of these is the fragmentation of the working population that results from the reduction in stable, decently paid jobs, producing a society that is split into two main groups: stable, full-time workers and those on temporary contracts or unemployed. Some supporters of this dual model claim that the same thing happened at the beginning of the industrial revolution. Initially, it led to a deterioration in the living conditions of large sections of the population, but in the long run it contributed greatly to their improvement. These claims conveniently ignore the fact that conquests such as the eight-hour day were not the automatic consequence of technological progress but the result of social struggles.

The prioritization of intellectual resources in the information society means that cultural factors have great importance. On the other hand, as a consequence of the dual model of society, education, which supplies the resources that reinforce the barriers between the three sectors of the population, is becoming an increasingly important criterion for determining who joins which group. The educational curriculum, therefore, has become a factor in the process of social dualization, the selection of the fittest, a situation that Jürgen Habermas describes in the language of social Darwinism (1988, p. 36).

Increasingly, stable workers are those with a university degree, and the unemployed are those without an elementary level of education. Ideas such as overeducation, the university as a breeding ground of the unemployed, or young people as the most marginalized group in the workforce are all clearly false.[2] Only those with a good grasp of the currently prioritized knowledge find a place among the fully employed.

The Dissolution of the Values of Solidarity

The changes in society have challenged social reforms and the objectives of social movements that had achieved a considerable degree of strength by the 1960s, especially in southern European countries. Their success depended on the dissolution of three things:

1. The emancipatory perspective of movements and reforms whose egalitarian orientation opposed the changes being promoted. These were described as outdated—as nostalgia for 1968.
2. The concept of the transforming social subject, which underpinned the idea of the vanguard organization in social movements and of the state as guarantor of its citizens' welfare. This subject was identified as the cause of all social evils and as invested with totalitarian tendencies.
3. The social sciences and the practices associated with them. These had developed alongside the welfare state policies that were now being questioned. They were attacked by a relativism that claimed that things were not true or false, good or bad.

Neoliberalism used every resource available to achieve its objectives. Intellectuals and their work were not exempt from this process. On the contrary, a large number of writers and lines of thought have participated in the struggle against emancipatory movements.

The Closed Circle of Educational Inequality

Great social transformations usually result in the marginalization of large sections of the population. The marginalization associated with the transition from the industrial society to the information society has an important cultural element. The knowledge prioritized by the new forms of life is distributed unevenly among individuals, according to social group, gender, ethnic group, and age. At the same time, the knowledge possessed by marginalized groups is dismissed, even if it is richer and more complex than prioritized knowledge. More is therefore given to those who have more and less to those who have less, forming a closed circle of cultural inequality. We can identify three types of phenomena in this process: distinction, imitation, and colonization.

Distinction

Those groups that occupy privileged social positions also have the symbolic power to decide what is culturally valuable. Their decisions are determined both by what is functional for social development and by what allows them to remain the sole holders of the knowledge in question (see Bourdieu, 1979, for a different but important perspective). The information society, the increasingly hegemonic dual model, and the glorification of the individual and diversity have intensified the phenomenon of distinction in sociocultural practices. Privileged groups increasingly choose their cultural habits for their symbolic power in order to differentiate themselves from the rest of society.

The relationship between beauty and skin color illustrates what is happening in our cultural and social life. Formerly, in Spain and other European countries, the whiter a person's skin, the more attractive they were held to be, and if privileged groups went to the beach, they did so with a sunshade. At that time, many people lived or worked in the open air and normally had dark complexions. However, during the period of rapid economic development after World War II, more and more people began to work in factories, shops, and offices. Privileged groups who had previously wanted to stay as white as possible began to buy houses on the seashore and to cultivate a tan, since this was a sign of their leisure and was now considered attractive. In recent years, when almost everyone could sunbathe at the beach, another skin coloring has come to be seen as even more attractive: a ski tan. And if it includes the mark of the ski goggles, all the better.

We can see an extraordinary acceleration of this process in all areas of our social and cultural lives. Albinoni's *Adagio* used to be considered a piece of music for aristocrats or melancholics. In the 1970s it began to be played on the radio, and an appreciation for it spread. Now, in select circles it is considered slightly vulgar, in the same way as Vivaldi's *Four Seasons*; and other less accessible pieces, such as Bach's *The Well-Tempered Clavier*, are more valued.

Imitation

The magic of status leads large numbers of people to choose their sociocultural practices in unconscious imitation of privileged groups. This process is doubly prejudicial to those involved. On the one hand, imitation entails a devaluation of their own culture in exchange for a facsimile of practices that are valued for their differentiating power. When the "beautiful people" in Madrid decided to take up dancing the Sevillanas, after the PSOE won the elections in 1982 led by a group of politicians from Seville, what they learned in their classes was more a mechanical one, two, three, four than the spirit of the dance. On the other hand, imitation involves the pursuit of an objective that, by definition, is unreachable. When everyone can go to the beach, even if only on Sundays and crammed into a train with hundreds of others, the definition of attractiveness is no longer a beach tan but a ski tan, which is much less accessible. The objective of integration that is part of the traditional current of modernity is therefore doubly negative for those groups who find themselves on the margins of society. First, it entails the expropriation of their own culture. Second, that expropriation does not lead to full integration into the adopted culture but to a secondary position within it.

This analysis questions the depth of the supposed flowering of diversity in the world today. The really novel feature of the present epoch in the frequency with which homogenization is experienced as diversity and individuality, as the possibility of programming time and its uses according to our individual tastes and characteristics. We find ourselves drawing up the curriculum for our own leisure time. We are immersed in a new cultural model exemplified by the individualized dolls designed by Roberts, which are "adopted" with their own birth certificates. Each boy and girl, therefore, has a unique toy, different from all the rest but nevertheless profoundly the same. We could characterize this model by paraphrasing the Lampedusa principle: "Everyone must feel different, so that everyone is the same."

Colonization

Educational activities that are theoretically designed to promote the democratization of culture are often imprisoned within the systemic dynamic that dominates our principle educational institutions. Processes of bureaucratization and academicization are not limited to the school system; they are also present in the participants and professionals who take part in other cultural practices. Frequently, the curricular designs of community workers are as directive as those of the schools that they claim to reject—as in the dance classes cited above. An academic structure is useful in some forms of learning. However, many other cultural activities require a very different structure. If the scope of its activity is not limited, the official curriculum generates an engineering mentality that regiments the lifeworld.[3] Even the most intimate and recreational areas of an individual's life can be colonized by invasive, totalizing practices in the form of institutionalized courses of ballroom dancing, massage, or even flirting and kissing. The important thing is not the institutional framework in which these courses take place but the practices they generate.

Guaranteeing the universal right to culture entails a struggle against the engineering mentality, which is colonizing our social and private lives and is deeply rooted in the cultural institutions of modernity.

Cultural intervention, precisely because it has greater institutional flexibility than the school system, can contribute to this decolonization. But one prerequisite is that it commits itself to a general project that includes opposition to any academicism in the definition of the culture it promotes as a right.

Traditional, Postmodern, and Communicative Perspectives on Current Educational Inequalities

Traditional Modernity

Traditional modernity bases itself on the division between the transforming subject and the transformed object: the teacher-subject who imparts culture to the student-object, the party-subject that raises the consciousness of the worker-object, the society-subject that exploits the nature-object. The current crisis of modernity has delegitimized these subjects and the absolute truths (culture, emancipation, truth, progress) on which they are based.

For those who take a traditional view of modernity, its institutions are the guarantee of universal access to the world of culture. All we need do is correct their imperfections, bring them up to date, and improve the quality of the services they offer. This perspective includes the conservative current of thought that considers culture as something already created by specific social groups, institutions, and disciplines and that assigns a passive role to the majority, who assimilate the culture. But it also includes reformist opinion, which advocates improving the present institutions, as if their potential were infinite, therefore denying the reality of their limits and the need to create new social spaces. The conservative current experiences the crisis as nostalgia for some supposed time when the official culture was respected by the institutions of modernity and by society as a whole. It alternative consists of returning this model to its former prestige, restoring the authority of teachers, guaranteeing the presence of time-honored values in the school curriculum, eliminating those elements in the mass media and other forms of cultural expression that "degrade" our culture.

The new North American cultural right has taken the lead in these arguments. Writers such as Allan Bloom (1987) and Eric Donald Hirsch (1987) claim that the solution to the present educational crisis lies in schools occupying themselves less with freedom and more with "truth." They consider pedagogical renewal, the democratization of school life, and inadequate teacher training as the cause of falling standards.

The Nietzschean Rebellion against Modernity

Postmodern, genealogical, and deconstructionist approaches of a Nietzschean variety are currently at the forefront of the rebellion against the emancipatory objectives of modernity through the dissolution of the transformative subject.[4] The antidemocratic, antiegalitarian work of Nietzsche has become the inspiration for an attack on critical postures and cooperative values. His pedagogical model of the Schopenhauerian man (Nietzsche, 1964) claims that individuals must continually create themselves by struggling against social pressures. The principles of social cohabitation and the consensus that exists around them form part of the social pressure that hampers rebellion. Nietzsche sees in the advance of modernity a decline in the vitality needed for individuals to surpass themselves. He cites the objectives of modern democratic societies, and especially those of utopian or emancipatory social movements (human rights, pacifist, feminist), as the causes of this decline. Among those things he identifies as negative are "the coming of democracy, of peace arbitrages instead of wars, of women rights equality" (Nietzsche, 1956, pp. 290–91).

Their opposition to modernity and its utopian and emancipatory dimension has turned these currents of thought into an effective intellectual weapon against perspectives, such as social movements and the policies of the welfare state, that oppose the increasing inequality of the dual model of the information society. In the area of education, Nietzschean writers oppose transformative perspectives, social movements, and proposals for pedagogical renewal. As the African American intellectual Cornel West says, "the foucaultian model of black postmodern as skeptic intellectual . . . provides a sophisticated excuse for ideological and social distance from insurgent black movements for liberation . . . encapsulates black intellectual activity within the comfortable bourgeois academy of postmodern America" (1993, pp. 79–82).

The error that many critical educators make when they follow these writers sometimes originates in their reading secondhand versions that, in turn, are based on superficial readings of the original works. For example, the work of Foucault is often cited as a useful tool to alert educators against the negative effects of power (Ball, 1990), although on various occasions (Levy, 1977; Foucault, 1975), Foucault himself insists, following Nietzsche, that power does not produce exclusion or repression but, rather, positive consequences.[5]

The Communicative Perspective

In opposition to both the traditional subject–object division and the reactionary dissolution of the transformative subject, the communicative perspective conceives of all individuals as subjects through their participation in intersubjective dialogue. This perspective is based on new theoretical developments in the social sciences (Habermas, 1984, 1989a; Giddens, 1991, 1992) and uses the dialogic and transformative elements of various educational theories and practices to develop new critical approaches that oppose inequality. (Some transformative educational theories have always emphasized dialogue; see Freire, 1970.) The perspective proposes the search for a nonhomogenizing educational equality that includes the equal right of each individual and group to develop their own difference. The new social theories are dual in conception: system and lifeworld (Habermas) or structure and agency (Giddens).[6] They therefore contemplate the possibility of dialogue and transformation on the part of groups and individuals, an advance over the conservative immobilism of the structuralist cultural reproduction model and the poststructuralist position of Nietzschean theorists.

The communicative perspective identifies the need for critical and transformative interventions that develop communicative theories and practices aimed at overcoming the inequalities created by the dual model of the information society. But these transformations cannot be imposed by a subject that considers itself in possession of the truth. The necessary changes must be defined through dialogue and consensus among all the parties involved. This search for consensus will involve participants with very unequal power positions. Even though this option is better than the only other available possibility (imposition by the most powerful), a critical approach must invent ways of moving toward more egalitarian consensuses. This is where the indispensable role of the social movement lies.[7]

Multiculturalism: Ethnocentric, Relativist, and Communicative Approaches to Relations between Cultures

Terminology

The following terms are used in a wide variety of ways in different societies, cultures, and schools of thought and even by different individuals within those schools. It is therefore impossible to produce a single agreed-upon set of definitions. The following should therefore be taken only as a suggested classification, used by various writers on the topic but with no pretentions to universal validity.

Multiculturalism is understood as the recognition that a number of cultures coexist in the same geographical area. *Interculturalism* is a form of intervention in this reality, which emphasizes the relationship between the cultures. *Pluriculturalism* is another form of intervention, which emphasizes the preservation of each culture's identity. *Intercultural education* favors the coexistence of members of different ethnic groups in the same school and sees single-culture schools as ghettos. *Pluricultural* education favors institutions that allow students to preserve and develop their own culture. For example a Gypsy school in Barcelona would be seen as a ghetto from an interculturalist point of view and an opportunity for the preservation of cultural identity from a pluriculturalist point of view.[8]

The Ethnocentric Approach: Interculturality as Assimilation or Integration

The perspective of traditional modernity adopts an ethnocentric approach. It establishes one culture as dominant because it is considered superior or the original and proper culture of a nation or geographical area. This identification then, explicitly or implicitly, forms the basis for the annihilation of the other cultures. Advocates of this approach claim to oppose schools based on other cultures or the inclusion of elements of those cultures in the curriculum because of the danger of erecting barriers and promoting marginalization. However, their elitism shows itself when they fail to oppose French- or German-language schools or the continual incorporation of elements from English-speaking cultures into Latin cultures.

The most explicit and conservative versions of ethnocentrism are xenophobia and racism, which oppose the very fact of multiculturality. They are based on the idea that each ethnic group or culture should remain in its own "homeland." Various methods are used to achieve this, from institutional exclusion, to preventing immigrants from entering the country, to violence in the form of physical attack on those already living there.

In the versions of this perspective that accept multiculturality up to a point, intercultural education is proposed as a way of achieving assimilation or integration. This involves welcoming members of other cultures and helping them to acquire the dominant culture. This ethnocentric approach maintains and reproduces existing inequalities, even when it claims not to be racist because it takes no account of skin color or racial origin when grading individuals in a class or choosing them for a job. This is because it accepts, often unconsciously, the false neutrality of the dominant culture—the rules of the game. Put another way, if the educational system is a white, male, European creation, and we believe it should continue to be based on that form of culture, it is understandable that most students from other cultures fail within it, and those who succeed do so only at the cost of renouncing their identity.

The Relativist Approach: Pluriculturalism to Preserve Identities

Nietzschean perspectives tend to adopt relativist positions (Foucault, 1992). They begin by questioning the modern principles of universal liberty, equality, and fraternity. Relations between cultures within the framework of modernity are understood as a destruction of cultures, identities, people, and individuals. Schools are seen as a key weapon in this process. From this starting point, the impossibility of an open dialogue between cultures is proclaimed, thus ruling out any attempt at intervention, valorization, or even analysis that is not made from within the culture itself. This leads to an emphasis on the preservation and development of cultural identities.

Within the terminological classification adopted here, this approach allows room for only pluriculturality, as all intercultural action hides ethnocentrism because it cannot take place in the ideal conditions of a dialogue between equals. However, the advocacy of pluricultural education by this approach (and even more so, the occasional proposal of intercultural education) is contradictory, because the creation of educational systems and schools is itself a practice that originates in one form of culture.

In its coherent versions, the relativist approach tends to reproduce, and even intensify, existing inequalities by ignoring the fact that these do not originate only in the relations between cultures established in modernity but also in the characteristics of each of the cultures themselves. There are profound inequalities among individuals in all cultures along a wide range of variables, such as gender and age. These inequalities will not be overcome by preserving the identity of each culture so that it cannot evolve. And it is evolution that relativists fiercely oppose.

The Communicative Approach: Interculturalism and Pluriculturalism as Options in a Process of Open Dialogue toward Equality

The communicative perspective suggests an approach based on dialogue as a form of relations between cultures and as a way of combating exclusions and inequality (Habermas, 1989b; Wang et al., 1990). This perspective considers that the culture of modernity has led to the destruction of many cultures but that it has also spread liberating ideas and practices, such as the universal right to literacy regardless of age, gender, and ethnic group. It considers that homogeneity has excluded and destroyed cultural richness but that when equality has included respect for difference, the result has been egalitarian, helping to overcome many of the terrible exclusions that individuals and peoples suffered in premodernity.

The communicative approach claims that, to the maximum extent possible, decisions should be left in the hands of the individuals involved. It therefore sees the simultaneous existence of interculturality and pluriculturality as offering a greater range of options and therefore greater freedom. The existence of Spanish-language schools in New York means that many people have the opportunity to choose between attending a Spanish school or a more intercultural school—between giving priority to preserving their own culture or to acquiring the dominant culture. But the communicative approach is both critical of its social context and self-critical. It recognizes that in the present social conditions the dominant culture continues to be dominant in any educational project. However, it considers that ethnocentrism and relativism are two sides of the same coin and that they maintain and reinforce current inequalities. Dialogue does not enable these inequalities to be eliminated suddenly, but it does permit an advance toward their elimination.

The objective of this approach is to diminish exclusionary elements and increase egalitarian ones in relations between cultures, through dialogue. It therefore favors evolution and the rupture of cultural homogeneity, because all cultures, including the dominant one, are enriched by hybridization.

Between Diversity and Educational Inequality: Producing Exclusion and Producing Equality

Diversity as an Alternative to Equality

One of the key elements in many educational reforms is diversity, difference, choice, or other proposals that establishes separate curricular routes for different groups or individuals. This policy is supported by relativist arguments in favor of respect for different social contexts, individuals, and cultures. However, it ignores the fact that the society in which these educational reforms take place is unequal as well as diverse. This can mean that what actually happens in the name of adaptation to diversity is in fact adaptation to inequality, instead of an attempt to overcome it.

In an unequal society, the tendency is for different curricular routes to sanction and reinforce previously existing inequalities. A wide range of factors (economic possibilities, social expectations, family culture, the cultural arbitrariness of schools) ensure that these routes vary according to social class, gender, ethnic group, and age. When it is isolated from the unequal social context, the idea of diversity itself becomes one more of these factors.

If the objective is not to reach a common educational level for all but to accommodate a diversity of needs, ignoring the context of social inequality can lead to approval for different curricular routes that in fact represent different educational levels. For example, many private elite schools concentrate on competitive forms of education that prepare students for the higher levels of the educational system and society, but the priority of many poor neighborhood public schools is to make sure their students pass the time as peacefully as possible while they try to teach them something. When this happens, we are doing no more than adapting students from a young age to the new inequalities of the information society, from the highly qualified, well-paid, and socially integrated professionals to the structurally unemployed on the margins of society. Reaching the top rungs on this ladder requires a highly competitive education. The lower rungs require habituation so that this situation is accepted without aggression.

This attitude focuses on adaptation to the environment and what are considered the unequal abilities of the students. Sometimes it is legitimized using transformative theories such as Lev Semenovich Vygotsky's, duly reinterpreted from a conservative point of view. Vygotsky (1986) relates cognitive development to its social context in a way that is relevant to sociocultural transformations. However, many people use this idea not to push for changes in the social context that would permit better cognitive development but to adapt that development to existing conditions.

Unequal Homogeneity against Diversity

The only objective that unites the various sections of the right on the question of culture is the steady increase of privileges based on educational inequality. From among the plurality of available options, each group defends what it considers best represents its interests in each temporal and spatial context. Following the emphasis on diversity, the new cultural right has launched a counteroffensive around a defense of what it considers Culture, with a capital C. Cultural relativism, the communicative perspective, pedagogical renewal, inadequate teacher training, school democratization, and positive discrimination are all identified as causes of falling educational standards. This offensive initially took root in the countries of the center but is slowly spreading out toward the periphery.

The authors of *The Closing of the American Mind* (Bloom, 1987) and *Cultural Literacy* (Hirsch, Kett, and Tuefil, 1988) are the intellectual leaders of this offensive in the United States. Richard Rorty (1989, p. 200) thinks it is important to distinguish between Bloom's Straussian doubts about democracy and Hirsch's Deweyan desire for a better educated electorate. He disagrees with Bloom's notion that higher education should enable students to acquire the natural superiority of leading intellectual figures, but he agrees with Hirsch that children in the United States are not being given a secondary education that prepares them to carry out their role as citizens in a democracy. However, both of these writers defend a homogeneous conception of a sexist, ethnocentric, classist, and ageist culture. Both draw a line between culture and nonculture, with the former identified as that of upper-middle-class men of European descent who reach high levels of academic achievement in preadulthood.[9] It is important to note that this offensive does not oppose a diversity that leads to exclusion but rather the one that leads toward equality.

This is clear in the case of Bloom, because his proposal centers on promoting the excellence of an elite and ensuring that their education is not obstructed by democratic trends that would contaminate them with the company or the subcultures of the masses. Hirsch wants to provide everyone with a homogeneous culture, ignoring the fact that his choice among the various cultural possibilities marginalizes those who are not male, middle or upper class, preadult, and of European descent. (For a detailed analysis of Hirsch's work, see Donaldo Macedo, this volume.)

Equality that Includes Diversity

Equality is a more general objective than diversity, difference, and choice. Equality includes the right of everyone to choose to be different and to be educated in their own difference. When an emphasis on diversity obscures the objective of equality, consciously or unconsciously, this works in favor of exclusion. When diversity is attacked in the name of equality, the result is the unequal consumption of a homogeneous model of culture. The struggle for equality aims to overcome current educational and cultural inequalities, which in the information society play an increasingly important role in the reproduction and preservation of other social inequalities. This is not a question of ensuring equal access to a homogeneous culture but rather of redistributing human and material resources so that no one occupies an inferior position because they lack specific cultural characteristics. Paulo Freire has combined these two apparently contradictory elements in his proposal to start from a particular culture but to then move on to achieve a complete command of that cultural reality (Flecha, 1989).

According to the new critical perspectives, this redistribution requires the mobilization of the tremendous human and cultural resources of those who are now excluded as failures. In reality, educational and social failure is the failure of an educational system and a society that can neither recognize nor make use of the cultural richness of different groups and individuals.[10] Compensatory and welfare policies based on deficit theories create negative expectations of education that become self-fulfilling prophesies. A positive view of participants' educational abilities and the provision of enough resources to develop them are part of the cultural struggle of the new critical movements.

Educational equality is only one aspect of the idea of social equality, which has inspired the efforts of a multitude of progressive movements and individuals all over the world. If this objective is reduced to equality of access to unequal positions in society, it becomes one more form of legitimizing inequality. If educational movements and cultural workers communicate with other social movements and sectors of society, rejecting the corporatism that turns schools in on themselves, we will be contributing to the struggle against educational and social inequality. In this new critical perspective, we need to develop alternative theories as well as practices. At a time when quality and excellence are the order of the day, we must not allow conservatives to set the pace. There is no need to choose between social commitment and scientific value. Many of the best educationalists (Freire), psychologists (Vygotsky), and sociologists (Habermas) have been and are committed to social transformation.

Too often practices or theories are dismissed because they are progressive and valued because they support the powerful. The writers and institutions that make these unscientific judgments, on the basis of supposed technical knowledge, are in fact attempting to use culture and education as barriers to produce inequality. These conservative perspectives have been destroying hope and demoralizing students, social movements, and teachers for too long. It is time to claim the right to be different from those who appear to have become so insensitive that they remain unmoved by the new inequalities. We need to imagine better worlds and better schools, not to impose them on others in a totalitarian way but to keep alive the utopian spark that today's leading social theorists (Habermas, 1988b; Giddens, 1990) consider essential in all progressive analysis. After these years of disorientation, we can begin to construct new critical perspectives in theory and practice that, to paraphrase Jesse Jackson on the twenty-fifth anniversary of the assassination of Martin Luther King, keep our dreams alive.

Notes

1. A great many other names with the prefix *post* have also been used: Amitai Etzioni used the now fashionable term *postmodern*. Ralf Dahrendorf has referred to *postcapitalist* society. Other writers have used the adjectives *postbourgeois, posteconomic, postsocialist, postwelfare, postscarcity, postcivilized*.

2. According to the Survey of the Economically Active Population, between 1976 and 1992, the proportion of the working Spanish population dropped by 16 percent. This reduction was spread unevenly across educational achievement: 2 percent of those with higher education, 27 percent of those with an elementary level of education, and 55 percent of those classed as illiterate. In the shorter period between 1988 and 1992, the general figure fell by 2 percent, that for the higher education group rose by 8 percent, and the figures for the other two groups fell by 7 percent and 17 percent, respectively. These differences are important if we bear in mind that 46 percent of the occupied active population (5,583,800 workers) only have an elementary level of schooling or below; 13 percent (1,600,700) have higher- or prehigher-level qualifications.

3. In analyzing the rules of pedagogic discourse, Basil Bernstein (1990) demonstrates why carpentry is one thing and woodwork is another. And as P. Berger and H. Kellner (1981, pp. 131–33) point out: "Human life contains a rich, powerful reality, which resists absorption into the 'engineering mentality.' Sexuality, parenthood, marriage, and all the joys, sorrows and terrors of human existence are such that they will, ever again, break through the fragile constructions by which 'social engineers' try to constrain and rationalize them."

4. The Nietzschean writers I refer to are as follows: postmodern, Lyotard (1979); deconstructionist, Derrida (1967); genealogical, Foucault (1968). This analysis is not applicable to those writers who try to use elements of these approaches for critical, transformative, and even emancipatory purposes. Elsewhere (Giroux and Flecha, 1992, pp. 172–74), I analyze the causes of the difference between European postmodernism and its acceptance in the United States, a subject also discussed by Descombes (1987) and Rorty (1991). Habermas (1987) criticizes in depth the rebellions against the emancipatory objectives of modernity. Foucault's objective is to oppose any analysis from the left (1966, p. 354).

5. The present climate of intellectual confusion produces situations that weaken the cultural opposition to fascism. Critical educators fiercely defend the work of Nietzscheans such as Heidegger, who was not only a leading representative of Nazism, even after that regime had disappeared, but went as far as to identify the Führer with the *Dasëin* of the people. There are also educa-

tors, including feminists, who argue in support of Foucault, whose asocial concept of sexuality (1976, 1984a, 1984b) led him to advocate the decriminalization of rape (Cooper et al., 1977).

6. Their theories therefore move us beyond the decades of dominance by Parsonian structural functionalism (Parsons, 1951a, 1951b) and its derivatives, such as Levi-Strauss's structuralism. The cultural reproduction model is based on structuralism.

7. The critics of Habermas's notion of consensus forget (or are unaware) that civil disobedience plays a very important role in his model (Habermas, 1992).

8. A Gypsy school is here taken to mean a school in which the education is based on Gypsy culture, within the limits imposed by the school framework. It does not refer to a school in which non-Gypsy students cannot enroll.

9. One of the most important practical examples of ageism is the increased inequality produced by the current model of educational development. By prolonging and increasing the quality of basic, obligatory education and concentrating new provision in preadult years, an increasing number of adults find themselves below the new level.

10. In recent years, Silvia Scribner and others have carried out important research on the cognitive richness of nonacademic cultures (Martin and Scribner, 1991; Scribner, 1988).

References

Ball, S. J. 1990. *Foucault and Education: Disciplines and Knowledge*. London: Routledge.

Berger, Peter L., and Hansfried Kellner. 1981. *Sociology Reinterpreted: An Essay on Method and Vocation*. Garden City: Anchor Press/Doubleday.

Bernstein, Basil. 1990. *Poder, educación y conciencia. Sociología de la transmisión cultural*. Barcelona: Roure.

Bloom, Allan. 1987. *The Closing of the American Mind: How Higher Education Has Failed Democracy and Impoverished the Souls of Today's Students*. New York: Simon and Schuster.

Bourdieu, Píerre. 1979. *La distinction: critique sociale du jugement*. Paris: Les Éditions de Minuit. English translation, Harvard University Press, Cambridge, 1984.

Copper, C., J. P. Faye, M. O. Faye, M. Foucault, and M. Zecca. 1977. "Dialogue sur l'enfermement et la répression psychiatrique." *Change* 32/33:76–110. English translation in L. Kritzman, ed., *Michel Foucault: Politics, Philosophy, Culture. Interviews and Other Writings 1977–1984* (New York: Routledge, 1988).

Derrida, Jacques. 1967. *De la Grammatologie*. Paris: Editions de Minuit. English translation published by John Hopkins University Press, Baltimore, 1976.

Descombes, Vincent. 1987. "Je m'en Foucault." *London Review of Books* 9:20–21.

Flecha, Ramón. 1989. "Dialogando con Paulo Freire." *Temps d'Educació* 1:302–5.

Foucault, Michel. 1966. *Les mots et les choses. Un archéologie des sciences humaines*.

Paris: Gallimard. English translation published by Random House, New York, 1973.

———. 1968. *Nietzsche, la Généalogie et l'Histoire*. Paris: Presses Universitaires de France.

———. 1975. *Surveiller et punir. Naissance de la prison*. Paris: Gallimard. English translation published by Pantheon, New York, 1977.

———. 1976. *Histoire de la sexualité*. Vol. 1. *La volonté de savoir*. Paris: Gallimard. English translation published by Vintage, New York, 1978.

———. 1984a. *Histoire de la sexualité*. Vol. 2. *L' usage des plaisirs*. Paris: Gallimard. English translation published by Random House, New York, 1986.

———. 1984b. *Histoire de la sexualité*. Vol. 3. *Le souci de soi*. Paris: Gallimard.

———. 1992. *Genealogía del racismo. De la guerra de razas al racismo de Estado*. Madrid: La Piqueta. Lectures given in 1976–76.

Freire, Paulo. 1970. *The Pedagogy of the Oppressed*. New York: Herder and Herder.

Giddens, Anthony. 1990. "Modernity and Utopia." *New Statesman and Society* 3:20–22.

———. 1991. *Modernity and Self-Identity: Self and Society in the Late Modern Age*. Cambridge: Polity Press.

———. 1992. *The Transformation of Intimacy: Sexuality, Love, and Eroticism in Modern Societies*. Stanford: Stanford University Press.

Giroux, H. A., and R. Flecha. 1992. *Igualdad educativa y diferencia cultural*. Barcelona: Roure.

Habermas, Jürgen. 1984 (1981). *The Theory of Communicative Action*. Vol. 1. *Reason and the Rationalization of Society*. Boston: Beacon.

———. 1987 (1985). *The Philosophical Discourse of Modernity: Twelve Lectures*. Cambridge: MIT Press.

———. 1988a (1983). "Política conservadora, trabajo, socialismo y utopía." In *Ensayos políticos*. Madrid: Península.

———. 1988b (1984). "La crisis del estado del bienestar y el agotamiento de las energías utópicas." In *Ensayos políticos*. Madrid: Península. Lecture delivered to Spanish Parliament on November 26, 1984.

———. 1989a (1981). *The Theory of Communicative Action*. Vol. 2. *Lifeworld and System: A Critique of Functionalist Reason*. Boston: Beacon.

———. 1989b (1987–88). *Identidades nacionales y postnacionales*. Madrid: Tecnos.

———. 1992 (1986). "On Morality, Law, Civil Disobedience and Modernity." In *Autonomy and Solidarity: Interviews with Jürgen Habermas*. London: Verso.

Hirsch, Eric Donald, Jr., F. J. Kett, and J. Tuefil. 1988. *Dictionary of Cultural Literacy: What Every American Needs to Know*. Boston: Houghton Mifflin.

Levy, Bernard Henri. 1977. "Non au sexe roi." *Le nouvel observateur*, March 12.

Lyotard, Jean François. 1979. *La condition postmoderne. Rapport sur le savoir*. París: Les éditions de minuit. English translation published by University of Minnesota Press, 1984.

Martin, L., and S. Scribner. 1991. "Laboratory for Cognitive Studies of Work: A Case Study of the Intellectual Implications of a New Technology." *Teachers College Record* 92:582–602.

Nietzsche, Friedrich. 1956 (1887). "The Genealogy of Morals." In *The Birth of Tragedy and the Genealogy of Morals*. New York: Anchor Books Doubleday.

———. 1964 (1874). "Schopenhauer as Educator." In *The Complete Works of Friedrich Nietzsche*. Vol. 5. New York: Rusell and Rusell.

Parsons, T. 1951a. *The Social System*. Glencoe: Free Press.

———. 1951b. *Toward a General Theory of Action*. Cambridge: Harvard University Press.

Rorty, Richard. 1989. "Education without Dogma: Truth, Freedom, and Our Universities." *Dissent* (Spring): 198–204.

———. 1991. "Moral Identity and Private Autonomy: The Case of Foucault." *Essays on Heidegger and Others*. Cambridge: Cambridge University Press.

Scribner, S. 1988. *Head and Hand: An Action Approach to Thinking*. New York: Columbia University, National Center on Education and Employment. ERIC Document Reproduction Service no. CE 049 897.

Vygotsky, Lev S. 1986 (1934). *Thought and Language*. Cambridge: MIT Press.

Wang, K., M. T. Díaz, M. Engel, G. Grande, M. L. Martín, M. Pérez Serrano, and M. Martin. 1990. *Mujeres gitanas ante el futuro*. Madrid: Editorial Presencia Gitana.

West, Cornel. 1993. *Keeping Faith: Philosophy and Race in America*. New York: Routledge.

3

Education and Community
Involvement

Paulo Freire

In approaching education and community involvement, it seems fundamental to keep a certain distance from it in order to get to its substantiveness, its deepest significance. In the final analysis, considerations and analyses of the relationships between community involvement and educational practice start with a critical understanding of both. Such considerations and analyses should focus on how we become obligated, when practicing education with a progressive perspective, to engender participation in the educational practice by anyone connected with educational work, directly or indirectly.

Let us leave the understanding of a particular variety of educational practice, the progressive one, for later, and let us now inventory the aspects of educational practice that are present whether that practice is progressive or whether it is meant to maintain the status quo, whether it is neoliberal, postmodern conservative, or postmodern progressive. What is of concern now is to identify certain fundamental cores that enable us to say, This is not an educational practice. This is an educational practice.

The first aspect to emphasize is that educational practice is a necessary dimension of social practice (as are productive, cultural, and religious practices). As a social practice, education, in all its richness and complexity, is a phenomenon typical of our existence and thus is exclusively human. For this reason, also, educational practice is by nature historical. Species is not the all-determining point in the trajectory of human existence. As they invented existence, with the "materials" that life offered them, men and women invented or discovered all the possibilities that freedom implies, a freedom they did not receive but had to create and fight for. They are undeniably programmed beings, but as François Jacob (1991) points out, "programmed to learn," and thus are curious beings, a characteristic without which they could not know. Thus, men and women take risks, venture, and educate themselves in the game of freedom.

Had it not been for the invention of language, none of this would have been possible. On the other hand, language, which cannot exist in the absence of thought (although thought is possible without language) did not appear until the animal turned human. Loose, freed hands, working instruments for the hunt, hands that extend the body, thus expanding its range of action, played an undeniable role in the social construction of language. It has been a long time since Sollas said, "The work realized by hands is the materialization of thought" (Montagu, p. 3). There is no doubt that language developed and develops while things are being done by individuals, for themselves or for others, in cooperation. It is necessary, however, to recognize that the use and creation of tools were not enough nor was work that was not isolated. Other animals use tools, and what is more, hunt together, but that does not enable them to speak. "The activity specific to human beings," says Josef Schubert, "is the cooperative use of tools in the production of food and other goods" (p. 61). And, for that, language became necessary.

It was through reinventing themselves, experiencing or suffering the tense relationship between what they inherited and what they received or acquired from the social context—which they create and which created them—that human beings gradually became these beings who need to continue being in order to be, these historical and cultural beings who cannot be explained solely on the basis of biology or genetics or culture. Human beings cannot be explained exclusively on the basis of their conscience, as if instead of having been socially constituted and having transformed their bodies into conscious bodies, conscience became the all-powerful creator of the world around them. Nor can human beings be explained as the mere result of the transformations that take place in this world. These are beings who live, within themselves, the dialectics of the social, without which they could not be, and the individual, without which they would become dissolved into the social, without a mark, without a profile.

These historical and social beings that men and women are—conditioned but capable of recognizing themselves as such and thus able to overcome the limits of their very conditioning, programmed beings but "programmed to learn"—they necessarily have had to surrender to the experience of teaching and learning. The organization of their production, the education of their younger generations, their reverence for their dead, as well as their astonishment before the world, before their fears, and before their dreams, which are some sort of artistic "writing" about their reality, one they "read," long before the invention of writing; or their ever-present attempts to decipher the mysteries of the world through divination, through magic, and later, through science; all that would follow men and women as their creation and as an instigation to more learning, to more teaching, to more knowing.

Let us now focus on educational practice itself, such as we realize it today, and let us try to detect within it the signs that characterize it as educational practice. Let us seek to identify its fundamental components, those in the absence of which there is no educational practice. In simple fashion, schematic indeed, but not simplistic, we can say that every educational situation implies the following:

- The presence of individuals. The individual who, by teaching, learns and the individual who, by learning, teaches. Educator and learner.
- Objects of knowledge to be taught by teachers (educators) and to be apprehended by students (learners), so that they can learn them. Content.
- Mediate and immediate objectives, which direct or orient educational practice. This need to go beyond its own moment of action or the moment when it happens—educational directiveness—does not allow for neutrality in educational practice, demanding from educators a stand on their ethics, their dream, which is political. For this reason, for being impossibly neutral, educational practice presents educators with the imperative of deciding, thus of breaking away, and of opting for tasks for participating subjects and not for manipulated objects.
- Methods and processes, teaching techniques, teaching materials, which must be coherent with the objectives and with the political option, with the utopia and with the dream that impregnates the educational project in question.

If human beings had not become capable of choosing, deciding, breaking away, and projecting, capable of remaking themselves as they remake the world, due, among other reasons, to the invention of conceptual language; if they had not become capable of valuation, of dedication to the point of sacrifice to the dream they fight for, of singing and praising the world, of admiring beauty, there would be no reason for talking about the impossibility of neutrality in education. But there would not be any reason to talk about education, either. We speak of education because we are able, even as we practice it, to deny it. The exercise of freedom leads us to the need to make choices, and this need leads us to the impossibility of being neutral.

Well then, the total impossibility of being neutral before the world, before the future—which I do not understand as an inexorable time, a given fact, but rather as a time to be created through the transformation of the present, through which dreams also gradually become materialized—presents us with the right and the duty of positioning ourselves as educators. The duty of not omitting ourselves. The right and the duty to live our educational practice in a coherent fashion with our political options. That is how, if one opts for progressiveness, for substantive democracy, one must—while respecting the right of learners to choose and to learn how to choose, which they need freedom for—give them testimony of the freedom with which we too choose our options (or of the obstacles we may have found in doing so). And one must never attempt to (deceivingly or not) impose one's choices on them.

If we opt for democracy, and if we are coherent in that choice in such a way that our practice does not contradict our discourse, it is not possible for us to do a number of things not uncommonly done by people who proclaim themselves progressive. Let us consider some of them:

1. Not taking into account the experience-based, finished knowledge that learners come to school with, only valuing accumulated, so-called scientific, knowledge, which one possesses.
2. Taking the learner for the object of educational practice, when in fact they are its active subject. In this way, the learner is made to be the sole reflection of one's teaching action. In other words, one takes on the active subject role of teaching, transferring packaged knowledge to the learner, who then becomes the docile, thankful recipient of a package that must be memorized. To democratic educators, teaching is not this mechanical act of transferring to learners the conceptual profile of the object of knowledge. Teaching is, above all, making it impossible for learners, who are epistemologically curious, to gradually empower themselves to know the deeper significance of the object, to apprehend it. That is the only way to learn it.

    Teaching and learning are, to the coherent, progressive educator, moments in the broader process of discovery. For this very reason, they involve search, live curiosity, misunderstanding, understanding, mistakes, serenity, rigorousness, suffering, and tenacity; but also satisfaction, pleasure, and happiness (see, to this end, Snyders, 1986).

3. To loudly defend the position that whoever thinks differently—that is, whoever respects the knowledge the learner brings to school, not to keep revolving around it but to go beyond it—is a populist, licentious focalist.
4. To defend the narrow view of school as an exclusive space for "lessons to be taught and lessons to be learned," thus having to be kept immune from the struggles, the conflicts, that take place "far away" from it, in a distant world. After all, a school is not a union.
5. To hyperinflate one's authority to the point of drowning the learner's freedom, meeting any attempt to rebel on their part with reinforced authoritarianism.
6. Constantly taking intolerant positions in which coexistence with the different is impossible. It is not possible to grow within intolerance. The coherently progressive educator knows that being excessively certain of one's positions may lead them to consider that outside those there is no salvation. The intolerant are authoritarian and messianic. For this reason they help the development of democracy in nothing.
7. To base one's search for the qualitative improvement of education in the creation of content "packages," to which are added manuals or guides addressed to teachers on the use of such packages.

It is easy to realize that such practices reek with authoritarianism. On the one hand, they denote no respect for the critical abilities of teachers, their knowledge, their practice. On the other hand, there is the arrogance with which half a dozen specialists who judge themselves enlightened develop these packages, which teachers, then, must tamely follow to the specifications of guides and manuals. One of the connotations of authoritarianism is total disbelief in the possibilities of others. The best that authoritarian leadership is capable of doing to preserve some semblance of democracy is their sparse attempts to hear the opinions of teachers about programs, but only when those are already being implemented. Instead of betting on the expertise of educators, authoritarianism banks on its own "proposals" and on subsequent evaluation, conducted with the purpose of determining whether the "packages" have been adhered to and properly followed.

From the point of view of coherently progressive, thus democratic, educators, things are quite different. Improvement in the quality of education implies the permanent development of teachers. And permanent development must be based on analyzing their practice. Only by thinking through their practice, naturally with the support of highly qualified personnel, is it possible for teachers to realize the theory built into their practice, whether this theory has been noticed, has been fully realized, or has been embraced.

Coherent, progressive educators cannot hesitate between "packages" and permanent development; they must always opt for development. They know all too well, among other things, that it is unlikely that critical thinking will be achieved by learners through the domestication of educators. How can educators provoke in the learner the critical curiosity necessary to the act of knowing, their taste for laughter and for creative adventure, if they do not trust themselves, do not take risks, if they are themselves tied to the "guide" from which "banking" concepts are to be transferred to the learners? This authoritarian form of betting on the packages rather than on the scientific, pedagogical, and political development of teachers reveals just how much authoritarians fear freedom, restlessness, doubt, uncertainty, dreaming; and how eager they are for immobilism. There is much necrophilia in the authoritarian, as much as there is biophilia in the democratically coherent progressive (see Fromm, 1980).

This said, I believe it is possible for us to begin a critical reflection about the issue of participation in general and community participation in particular.

The first observation that needs to be made is that participation—although an exercise in voice, in having voice, in involvement, in decision making at certain levels of power, although a right of citizenship—is in direct and necessary correlation to progressive educational practice, if the educators who realize it are coherent within their discourse. This is what I mean. It constitutes a glaring contradiction, a loud incoherence, to conceive of an educational practice that intends to be progressive but that is realized within such rigid, vertical models as to leave no room for the slightest doubt, for curiosity, criticism, suggestion, for a living presence, with a voice; an educational practice in which educators are subjected to packages; an educational practice whose learners are limited to studying without questioning, without doubting, subject to their teachers; an educational practice in which the school's other personnel—groundskeepers, cooks, security guards—are not also educators with a voice; an educational practice in which fathers and mothers are invited to the school only for end-of-year parties, or to hear complaints about their children, or to become involved as volunteers in repairing the school facilities, or even to "participate" in collections for the purchase of school materials. In these examples, we have complete prohibition or inhibition of participation or else false participation.

When I was education secretary for the city of São Paulo, being committed to creating an administration that, coherent with our utopia, took the issue of popular participation in the destiny of schools seriously, as it should, my team and I indeed had to begin from the beginning. In other words, we began by undertaking administrative reform so that the Department of Education could work in a different manner. It was impossible to create a democratic administration, one that was for the autonomy of public and popular schools, within an administrative structure that could only make viable authoritarian and hierarchical power. Such structures affected all, from the secretary to the immediate directors and department heads who, in turn, extended orders to the schools. In the schools, principals would then add their own demands to those orders, thus silencing the groundskeepers, guards, cooks, teachers, and students. Of course, there were always exceptions, without which the work of change would have proved excessively difficult.

It would not have been possible to bring the public school system up to the level of the challenges that Brazilian democracy presents us with in terms of learning by encouraging our society's authoritarian tradition. It was necessary, on the contrary, to democratize power, to recognize the right of students and teachers to a voice, to decrease the personal power of principals, and to create new venues of power, such as School Councils, which played both a decision-making and a consulting role and through which, first of all, mothers and fathers could gain involvement in the destinies of their children and of the school and which, secondly, could engender in the local community a sense of ownership of the school and make it active in the implementation of educational policy within the school.

It was thus necessary to democratize the Department of Education. It was necessary to decentralize decisions, to inaugurate a collegiate governance that limited the power of the secretary. It was necessary to redirect the teacher-development policy, overcoming the traditional summer teacher programs that focused on theoretical discourse and instituting a concern for discussion about their practice so as to enable teachers to put theory into practice. This is an effective way for us to live out the dialectic unity between theory and practice.

Something I want to make clear is that a greater level of democratic participation on the part of students, teachers, mothers, fathers, the local community, on the part of a school that, while public, intends to continually become popular, requires light structures, adaptable, decentralized structures, which allow for quick and effective government action. The heavy structures of centralized power, in which decisions that require speed drag along from department to department, waiting for approval here and there, are identified with and in the service of authoritarian, elitist, and above all, traditional administrations with a colonial flavor. Without the transformation of such structures, which

wind up profiling us to their image, there is no way to think about popular or community participation. Democracy requires democratizing
structures, rather than structures that inhibit an active presence of civil
society in the command of public things.

That is what we did. I must have become the education secretary for
the city of São Paulo with the least personal power, but for this reason,
I was able to work effectively and decide with others.

Recently, a graduate student (Margarite May Berkenbrock, whom I
thank for allowing me to cite her interviews) in the Supervision and
Curriculum Program at the Pontifical Catholic University of São Paulo
and who is working on a thesis titled "Popular Participation in the
School: Democratic Learning in the Country of Exclusions," heard the
following response from one of the mothers in a discussion group,
when she asked, "Do you think the School Council plays an important
role? Why?"

"Yes," the mother answered. "It is good because, in part, the community can find out what the school is like from the inside. What is
done with our children, how the money is used. Before, the community was kept outside the school gate. We would only come in the
school for grades and complaints about our children. In the old times,
that was all parents were called for—or to bring food to the parties.
With the councils, space was created for a parent," she continued, "as
they come into the school, to begin to learn about the school from the
inside. Through the council, we were able to provide lunch for the second grade, because their schedule didn't allow for having lunch at
home."

The resistance we had to face from principals, pedagogical coordina-
tors, and teachers who "hosted" in themselves the elitist, colonial authoritarian ideology! "What is this?" they would at times question,
somewhere between offended and surprised. "Will we now have to
put up with suggestions and criticism from these ignorant people who
know nothing about pedagogy?"

Ideology, whose death has been proclaimed but that remains quite
alive, with its power to dull reality and make us nearsighted, prevented them from realizing that the experiential knowledge of parents,
the first educators, had much to contribute to the growth of the school
and that the knowledge of teachers could help parents better understand problems experienced at home. Finally, the residue of authoritarianism would not allow them even to intuit the importance, toward the
development of our democratic process, of dialogue between those
knowledges and of an intimate, popular presence in the school. To the
authoritarian, democracy deteriorates whenever the popular classes
become too present in the schools, on the streets, out in public, de-

nouncing the ugliness of the world and announcing a more beautiful world.

I would like to conclude by reiterating that community involvement in the area I focused most on, school, in search of autonomy, must not imply omission on the part of the state. School autonomy does not imply the state escaping the responsibility of providing quality education in sufficient quantity to meet social demand. I reject certain neoliberal positions that, seeing everything the state does as perverse, defends a peculiar privatization of education. The idea is to privatize education but to have the state finance it. The government, then, would transfer funds to schools that would be organized by civil society leaders. Some popular groups have lent support to this position, without realizing the risk they are running: that of encouraging the state to wash its hands of one of its most serious obligations—commitment to popular education.

Popular groups certainly have the right to organize and create their own community schools and to fight to constantly improve them. They even have the right to demand that the state cooperate with them through nonpaternalistic cooperation agreements. They must be aware, however, that their mission is not to replace the state in its obligation to meet the educational needs of all in the popular classes and of those in the privileged classes who may seek out the public schools. Nothing should be done, therefore, in the direction of helping the elitist state to be excused from its obligations. On the contrary, within community schools or public schools, the popular classes need to fight hard for the government's fulfilling of its duty. The struggle of an autonomous school is not against a public school.

References

Fromm, Erich. 1980. *El Corazon del Hombre*. Vol. 21. The Heart of Man: Its Genius for Good and Evil. New York: Harper & Row.

Jacob, François. 1991. "Nous sommes programés, mais pour apprendre." *Le Courrier de l'Unesco* (February).

Montagu, Ashley. 1983. "Toolmaking, Hunting, and the Origin of Language." In Bruce Bain, ed., *The Sociogenesis of Language and Human Conduct*. New York: Plenum.

Schubert, Josef. 1983. "The Implications of Luria's Theories for Cross-Cultural Research on Language and Intelligence." In Bruce Bain, ed., *The Sociogenesis of Language and Human Conduct*. New York: Plenum.

Snyders, Georges. 1986. *La Joie à l'école*. Paris: PUF.

4

Border Youth, Difference, and Postmodern Education

Henry A. Giroux

The task is to get to grips with the "passage to postmodernity,"
which has opened up since the late 1960s and the end of the postwar boom in the global capitalist economy, to achieve an understanding of the emerging new culture of time and space, and related transformations in forms of knowledge and experience in the
(post)-modern world.

Barry Smart, *Modern Conditions*, p. 202

For many theorists occupying various positions on the political spec-
trum, the current historical moment signals less a need to come to grips
with the new forms of knowledge, experiences, and conditions that
constitute postmodernism than the need to writ its obituary. The signs
of exhaustion are in part measured by the fact that postmodernism has
gripped two generations of intellectuals who have pondered endlessly
over its meaning and implications as a "social condition and cultural
movement" (Jencks, 1992, p. 10). The "postmodern debate" has
spurred little consensus and a great deal of confusion and animosity.

The themes are, by now, well known: master narratives and traditions of knowledge grounded in first principles are spurned; philosophical principles of canonicity and the notion of the sacred have become suspect; epistemic certainty and the fixed boundaries of
academic knowledge have been challenged by a "war on totality" and
a disavowal of all-encompassing, single, worldviews; rigid distinctions
between high and low culture have been rejected by the insistence that
the products of the so-called mass culture, popular, and folk art forms
are proper objects of study; the Enlightenment correspondence between history and progress and the modernist faith in rationality, sci-

ence, and freedom have incurred a deep-rooted skepticism; the fixed and unified identity of the humanist subject has been replaced by a call for narrative space that is pluralized and fluid. And, finally, though far from complete, history is spurned as a unilinear process that moves the West progressively toward a final realization of freedom. (For a particularly succinct examination of the postmodern challenge to a modernist conception of history, see Vattimo, 1992, esp. chap. 1.)

While these and other issues have become central to the postmodern debate, they are connected through the challenges and provocations they provide to modernity's conception of history, agency, representation, culture, and the responsibility of intellectuals. The postmodern challenge constitutes a diverse body of cultural criticism, but it must also be seen as a contextual discourse that has challenged specific disciplinary boundaries in such fields as literary studies, geography, education, architecture, feminism, performance art, anthropology, and sociology (see Jencks, 1992; Natoli and Hutcheon, 1993; Docherty, 1993). Given its broad theoretical reach, its political anarchism, and its challenge to "legislating" intellectuals, it is not surprising that there has been a growing movement on the part of diverse critics to distance themselves from postmodernism.

While postmodernism may have been elevated to the height of fashion hype in both academic journals and the popular press in North America during the last twenty years, it is clear that a more sinister and reactionary mood has emerged, which constitutes something of a backlash. Of course, postmodernism did become something of a fashion trend, but such events are short-lived and rarely take any subject seriously. But the power of fashion and commodification should not be underestimated in terms of how such practices bestow on an issue a cloudy residue of irrelevance and misunderstanding.

But there is more at stake in the recent debates on postmodernism than the effects of fashion and commodification; in fact, the often essentialized terms in which critiques of postmodernism have been framed suggest something more onerous. In the excessive rhetorical flourishes that dismiss postmodernism as reactionary nihilism, fad, or simply a new form of consumerism there appears a deep-seated anti-intellectualism, one that lends credence to the notion that theory is an academic luxury and has little to do with concrete political practice. Anti-intellectualism aside, the postmodern backlash also points to a crisis in the way in which the project of modernity attempts to appropriate, prescribe, and accommodate issues of difference and indeterminacy.

Much of the criticism that now so blithely dismisses postmodernism appears trapped in what Zygmunt Bauman refers to as modernist "utopias that served as beacons for the long march to the rule of reason [which] visualized a world without margins, leftovers, the unaccounted for—without dissidents and rebels" (1992, p. xi). Against the indeterminacy, fragmentation, and skepticism of the postmodern era, the master narratives of modernism, particularly Marxism and liberalism, have been undermined as oppositional discourses. One consequence is that "a whole generation of postwar intellectuals have experienced an identity crisis. . . . What results is a mood of mourning and melancholia" (Mercer, 1992, p. 424).

The legacy of essentialism and orthodoxy seems to be reasserting itself on the part of intellectuals on the left, who reject postmodernism as a style of cultural criticism and knowledge production. It can also be seen in the refusal on the part of intellectuals to acknowledge the wide-ranging processes of social and cultural transformation taken up in postmodern discourses that are appropriate to grasping the contemporary experiences of youth and the proliferation of forms of diversity within an age of declining authority, economic uncertainty, the proliferation of electronically mediated technologies, and the extension of what I call consumer pedagogy into almost every aspect of the youth culture.

In what follows, I want to shift the terms of the debate in which postmodernism is usually engaged, especially by its more recent critics. In doing so, I argue that postmodernism as a site of "conflicting forces and divergent tendencies" (Patton, 1988, p. 89) becomes useful pedagogically when it provides elements of an oppositional discourse for understanding and responding to the changing cultural and educational shift affecting youth in North America. A resistant or political postmodernism seems invaluable in helping educators and others address the changing conditions of knowledge production in the context of emerging mass electronic media and the role these new technologies are playing as critical socializing agencies in redefining both the locations and the meaning of pedagogy.

My concern with expanding the way in which educators and cultural workers understand the political reach and power of pedagogy as it positions youth within a postmodern culture suggests that postmodernism is to be neither romanticized nor dismissed. On the contrary, it is a fundamentally important discourse, which needs to be mined critically in order to help educators to understand the modernist nature of public schooling in North America (Giroux, 1988, 1992). It is also useful for educators to comprehend the challenging conditions of identity formation within electronically mediated cultures and how they are producing a new generation of youth that exists between the borders of a modernist world of certainty and order, informed by the culture of the

West and its technology of print, and a postmodern world of hybridized identities, electronic technologies, local cultural practices, and pluralized public spaces.

But before I develop the critical relationship between postmodern discourse and the promise of pedagogy and its relationship to border youth, I want to comment further on the recent backlash against postmodernism and why I believe it reproduces rather than constructively addresses some of the pedagogical and political problems affecting contemporary schools and youth.

Welcome to the Postmodern Backlash

While conservatives such as Daniel Bell (1976) and his cohorts may see in postmodernism the worst expression of the radical legacy of the 1960s, an increasing number of radical critics view postmodernism as the cause of a wide range of theoretical excesses and political injustices. For example, recent criticism from the British cultural critic John Clarke (1991, esp. chap. 2) argues that the hyperreality of postmodernism wrongly celebrates and depoliticizes the new informational technologies and encourages metropolitan intellectuals to proclaim the end of everything in order to commit themselves to nothing (especially the materialist problems of the masses). (Clarke's analysis has little to do with a complex reading of postmodernism and more to with his own refusal to take seriously a postmodern critique of the modernist elements in Marxist theories.)

Dean MacCannell goes further, arguing that "postmodern writing [is] an expression of soft fascism" (1992, p. 187). The feminist theorist Susan Bordo dismisses postmodernism as just another form of "stylish nihilism" and castigates its supporters for constructing a "world in which language swallows up everything" (1993, p. 291). The backlash has become so prevalent in North America that the status of popular criticism and reporting seems to necessitate proclaiming that postmodernism is "dead." Hence, comments ranging from the editorial pages of the *New York Times* to popular texts such as *13thGen* to popular academic magazines such as the *Chronicle of Higher Education* alert the general public in no uncertain terms that it is no longer fashionable to utter the "p" word.

Of course, more serious critiques have appeared from the likes of Jürgen Habermas (1978), Perry Anderson (1984, 1998), David Harvey (1989), Terry Eagleton (1985), and Fredric Jameson (1998), but the current backlash has a different intellectual quality to it, a kind of reductionism that is both disturbing and irresponsible in its refusal to engage postmodernism in any kind of dialogical, theoretical debate.[1] Many of these left critics often assume the moral high ground and muster their theoretical machinery within binary divisions that create postmodern fictions on the one side and politically correct, materialist freedom fighters on the other. One consequence is that any attempt to engage the value and importance of postmodern discourses critically is sacrificed to the cold winter winds of orthodoxy and intellectual parochialism. I am not suggesting that all critics of postmodernism fall prey to such a position, not am I suggesting that concerns about the relationship between modernity and postmodernity, the status of ethics, the crisis of representation and subjectivity, or the political relevance of postmodern discourses should not be problematized. But viewing postmodernism as a terrain to be contested suggests theoretical caution rather than reckless abandonment or casual dismissal.

What is often missing from these contentious critiques is the recognition that, since postmodernism does not operate under any absolute sign, it might be more productive to reject any arguments that position postmodernism within an essentialized politics, an either/or set of strategies. A more productive encounter would attempt, instead, to understand how postmodernism's more central insights illuminate how power is produced and circulated through cultural practices that mobilize multiple relations of subordination.

Rather than proclaiming the end of reason, postmodernism can be critically analyzed for how successfully it interrogates the limits of the project of modernist rationality and its universal claims to progress, happiness, and freedom. Instead of assuming that postmodernism has vacated the terrain of values, it seems more useful to address how it accounts for how values are constructed historically and relationally and how they might be addressed as the basis or "precondition of a politically engaged critique" (Butler, 1991, pp. 6–7).

In a similar fashion, instead of claiming that postmodernism's critique of the essentialist subject denies a theory of subjectivity, it seems more productive to examine how its claims about the contingent character of identity, constructed in a multiplicity of social relations and discourses, redefines the notion of agency. One example of this type of inquiry comes from Judith Butler, who argues that acknowledging that "the subject is constituted is not [the same as claiming] that it is determined; on the contrary, the constituted character of the subject is the very precondition of its agency" (1991, p. 13). The now familiar argument that postmodernism substitutes representations for reality indicates less an insight than a reductionism that refuses to engage critically how postmodern theories of representation work to give meaning to reality (Lemert, 1997).

A postmodern politics of representation might be better served through an attempt to understand how power is mobilized in cultural terms, how images are used on a national and local scale to create a representational politics that is reorienting traditional notions of space and time. A postmodern discourse could also be evaluated through the pedagogical consequences of its call to expand the meaning of literacy by broadening "the range of texts we read, and . . . the ways in which we read them" (Berube, 1992–93, p. 75).

The fact of the matter is that the mass media play a decisive role in the lives of young people, and the issue is not whether such media perpetuate dominant power relations but how youth and others experience the culture of the media differently, or the ways media are "experienced differently by different individuals" (Tomlinson, 1991, p. 40). Postmodernism pluralizes the meaning of culture, while modernism firmly situates it theoretically in apparatuses of power. It is precisely in this dialectical interplay between difference and power that postmodernism and modernism inform each other rather than cancel each other. The dialectical nature of the relationship that postmodernism has to modernism warrants a theoretical moratorium on critiques that affirm or negate postmodernism on the basis of whether it represents a break from modernism. The value of postmodernism lies elsewhere.

Acknowledging both the reactionary and progressive moments in postmodernism, antiessentialist cultural work might take up the challenge of "writing the political back into the postmodern" (Ebert, 1991, 291), while simultaneously radicalizing the political legacy of modernism in order to promote a new vision of radical democracy in a postmodern world. One challenge in the debate over postmodernism is whether its more progressive elements can further our understanding of how power works, how social identities are formed, and how the changing conditions of the global economy and the new informational technologies can be articulated to meet the challenges posed by progressive cultural workers and the new social movements.

More specifically, the issue for critical educators lies in appropriating postmodernism as part of a broader pedagogical project, which reasserts the primacy of the political while simultaneously engaging the most progressive aspects of modernism. Postmodernism becomes relevant to the extent that it becomes part of a broader political project, in which the relationship between modernism and postmodernism becomes dialectical, dialogic, and critical.

In what follows, I want to illuminate and then analyze some of the tensions between schools as modernist institutions and the fractured conditions of a postmodern culture of youth, along with the problems they pose for critical educators. First, there is the challenge of understanding the modernist nature of existing schooling and its refusal to relinquish a view of knowledge, culture, and order that undermines the possibility for constructing a radical democratic project in which a shared conception of citizenship simultaneously challenges growing regimes of oppression and struggles for the conditions needed to construct a multiracial and multicultural democracy. Second, there is a need for cultural workers to address the emergence of a new generation of youth who are increasingly constructed within postmodern economic and cultural conditions that are almost entirely ignored by the schools. Third, there is the challenge to critically appropriate those elements of a postmodern pedagogy that might be useful in educating youth to be the subjects of history in a world that is increasingly diminishing the possibilities for radical democracy and global peace.

Modernist Schools and Postmodern Conditions

A clip from [the film] *War Games:* David Lightman (Matthew Broderick) sees a brochure of a computer company promising a quantum leap in game technology coming this Christmas . . . breaks into a system and, thinking it's the game company computer, asks to play global thermonuclear war. . . . Sees on TV that for three minutes Strategic Air Command went on full alert thinking there had been a Soviet sneak attack . . . is arrested and interrogated . . . breaks back into the system and asks the computer, "Is this a game or is it real?" The computer answers: "What's the difference?" (Parkes, 1994, p. 48)

Wedded to the language of order, certainty, and mastery, public schools are facing a veritable sea change in the demographic, social, and cultural composition of the United States, for which they are radically unprepared. As thoroughly modernist institutions, public schools have long relied upon moral, political, and social technologies that legitimate an abiding faith in the Cartesian tradition of rationality, progress, and history. The consequences are well known. Knowledge and authority in the school curricula are organized not to eliminate differences but to regulate them through cultural and social divisions of labor. Class, racial, and gender differences are either ignored in school curricula or subordinated to the imperatives of a history and culture that are linear and uniform. Within the discourse of modernism, knowledge draws its boundaries almost exclusively from a European model of culture and civilization and connects learning to the mastery of autonomous and specialized bodies of knowledge. Informed by modernist traditions, schooling becomes an agent of those political and intellectual technologies associated with what Ian Hunter (1988) terms the "governmentalizing" of the social order.

The result is a pedagogical apparatus regulated by a practice of ordering that views "contingency as an enemy and order as a task" (Bauman, 1992, p. xi). The practice of ordering, licensing, and regulating that structures public schooling is predicated on a fear of difference and indeterminacy. The effects reach deep into the structure of public schooling and include the following:

- An epistemic arrogance and faith in certainty sanctions pedagogical practices and public spheres in which cultural differences are viewed as threatening.
- Knowledge becomes positioned in the curricula as an object of mastery and control.
- The individual student is privileged as a unique source of agency irrespective of iniquitous relations of power.
- The technology and culture of the book is treated as the embodiment of modernist high learning and the only legitimate object of pedagogy.

While the logic of public schooling may be utterly modernist, it is neither monolithic nor homogeneous. But at the same time, the dominant features of public schooling are characterized by a modernist project that has increasingly come to rely upon instrumental reason and the standardization of curricula. In part, this can be seen in the regulation of class, racial, and gender differences through rigid forms of testing, sorting, and tracking. The rule of reason reveals its Western cultural legacy in a highly centered curriculum that more often than not privileges the histories, experiences, and cultural capital of largely white, middle-class students. Moreover, the modernist nature of public schooling is evident in the refusal of educators to incorporate popular culture into the curriculum or to take account of the new electronically mediated, informational systems in the postmodern age that are generating massively new socializing contexts for contemporary youth.

The emerging conditions of indeterminacy and hybridity that the public schools face but continue to ignore can be seen in a number of elements that characterize what I loosely call postmodern culture. First, the United States is experiencing a new wave of immigration that, by the end of this century, may exceed in volume and importance the last wave at the turn of the twentieth century. Key geographic areas within the country—chiefly large metropolitan regions of the Northeast and Southwest, including California—and major public institutions—especially those of social welfare and education—are grappling with entirely new populations that bring with them new needs. In 1940, 70 percent of immigrants came from Europe. In 1997, only 15 percent came from Europe, 44 percent came from Latin America, and 37 percent came from Asia. National identity can no longer be written through the lens of cultural uniformity or enforced through the discourse of assimilation. A new postmodern culture has emerged marked by specificity, difference, plurality, and multiple narratives.

Second, the sense of possibility that has informed the American Dream of material well-being and social mobility is no longer matched by an economy that can sustain such dreams. In the last two decades, the American economy has entered a prolonged era of stagnation, punctuated by short-term growth spurts. In the midst of an ongoing recession and declining real incomes for low- and middle-income groups, the prospects for economic growth over the next period of U.S. history appear extremely limited. The result has been the expansion of service economy jobs and an increase in the number of companies that are downsizing and cutting labor costs in order to meet global competition. Not only are full-time jobs drying up, but there has also been a surge in the "number of Americans—perhaps as many as 37 million—[who] are employed in something other than full-time permanent positions" (Jost, 1993, p. 633). These so-called "contingent workers" are "paid less than full-time workers and often get no health benefits, no pensions and no paid holidays, sick days or vacations" (p. 628).

Massive unemployment and diminishing expectations have become a way of life for youth all over North America. *MacLean's Magazine* reports that in Canada, "people ages 15 to 24 are currently facing unemployment rates of more than 20 percent, well above the national average of 10.8 percent" (Blythe, 1993, p. 35). For most contemporary youth, the promise of economic and social mobility no longer warrants the legitimating claims it held for earlier generations of young people. The signs of despair among this generation are everywhere. Surveys strongly suggest that contemporary youth from diverse classes, races, ethnicities, and cultures "believe it will be much harder for them to get ahead than it was for their parents—and are overwhelmingly pessimistic about the long-term fate of their generation and nation" (Howe and Strauss, 1993, p. 16).

Clinging to the modernist script that technological growth necessitates progress, educators refuse to give up the long-held assumption that school credentials provide the best route to economic security and class mobility. While such a truth may have been relevant to the industrializing era, it is no longer sustainable within the post-Fordist economy of the West. New economic conditions call into question the efficacy of mass schooling in providing the "well-trained" labor force that employers required in the past. In light of these shifts, it seems imperative that educators and other cultural workers reexamine the mission of the schools.

Rather than accepting the modernist assumption that schools should train students for specific labor tasks, it makes more sense in the present historical moment to educate students to theorize differently about the meaning of work in a postmodern world. Indeterminacy rather than order should become the guiding principle of a pedagogy in which multiple views, possibilities, and differences are opened up as part of an attempt to read the future contingently rather than from the perspective of a master narrative that assumes rather than problematizes specific notions of work, progress, and agency. Under such circumstances, schools need to redefine curricula within a postmodern conception of culture linked to the diverse and changing global conditions that necessitate new forms of literacy, a vastly expanded understanding of how power works within cultural apparatuses, and a keener sense of how the existing generation of youth are being produced within a society in which mass media plays a decisive if not unparalleled role in constructing multiple and diverse social identities.

As Stanley Aronowitz and I point out elsewhere:

> Few efforts are being made to rethink the *entire* curriculum in the light of the new migration and immigration, much less develop entirely different pedagogies. In secondary schools and community colleges, for example, students still study "subjects"—social studies, math, science, English and "foreign" languages. Some schools have "added" courses in the history and culture of Asian, Latin American, and Caribbean societies but have little thought of transforming the entire humanities and social studies curricula in the light of the cultural transformations of the school. Nor are serious efforts being made to integrate the sciences with social studies and the humanities; hence, science and math are still being deployed as sorting devises in most schools rather than seen as crucial markers of a genuinely innovative approach to learning. (1993, p. 6)

As modernist institutions, public schools have been unable to open up the possibility of thinking through the indeterminate character of the economy, knowledge, culture, and identity. Hence, it has become difficult, if not impossible, for such institutions to understand how social identities are fashioned and struggled over within political and technological conditions that have produced a crisis in the ways in which culture is organized in the West.

Border Youth and Postmodern Culture

The programmed instability and transitoriness characteristically widespread among a generation of eighteen-to-twenty-five-year-old border youth is inextricably rooted in a larger set of postmodern cultural conditions informed by the following assumptions:

- A general loss of faith in the modernist narratives of work and emancipation.
- The recognition that the indeterminacy of the future warrants confronting and living in the immediacy of experience.
- An acknowledgment that homelessness as a condition of randomness has replaced the security, if not misrepresentation, of home as a source of comfort and security.
- An experience of time and space as compressed and fragmented within a world of images that increasingly undermine the dialectic of authenticity and universalism.

For border youth, plurality and contingency, whether mediated through the media or through the dislocations spurred by the economic system, the rise of new social movements, or the crisis of representation have resulted in a world with few secure psychological, economic, or intellectual markers. This is a world in which one is condemned to wander across, within, and between multiple borders and spaces marked by excess, otherness, difference, and a dislocating notion of meaning and attention. The modernist world of certainty and order has given way to a planet in which hip-hop and rap condense time and space into what Paul Virilio (1991) calls "speed space." No longer belonging to any one place or location, youth increasingly inhabit shifting cultural and social spheres marked by a plurality of languages and cultures.

Communities have been refigured, as space and time mutate into multiple and overlapping cyberspace networks. Youth talk to each other over electronic bulletin boards in coffeehouses in North Beach, California. Cafes and other public salons, once the refuge of beatniks, hippies, and other cultural radicals, have given way to members of the hacker culture. They reorder their imaginations through connections to virtual reality technologies and lose themselves in images that wage a war on traditional meaning by reducing all forms of understanding to random access spectacles.

This is not meant to endorse a Frankfurt School dismissal of mass or popular culture in the postmodern age. On the contrary, the new electronic technologies with their proliferation of multiple stories and open-ended forms of interaction have altered not only the context for the production of subjectivities but also how people "take in information and entertainment" (Parkes, 1994, p. 54). Values no longer emerge from the modernist pedagogy of foundationalism and universal truths or from traditional narratives based on fixed identities and with their requisite structure of closure. For many youths, meaning is in rout, media has become a substitute for experience, and what constitutes understanding is grounded in a decentered and diasporic world of difference, displacement, and exchanges.

I take up the concept of border youth through a general analysis of some recent classic films that attempt to portray the plight of young people within the conditions of a postmodern culture, focusing on *River's Edge* (1986), *My Own Private Idaho* (1991), and *Slackers* (1991). All of these films point to some of the economic and social conditions at work in the formation of youth, but they often do so within a narrative that combines a politics of despair with a fairly sophisticated depiction of the sensibilities and moods of a generation of youth. The challenge for critical educators is to question how a critical pedagogy might be employed to cancel out the worst dimensions of postmodern cultural criticism while appropriating some of its more radical aspects. At the same time, there is the issue of how a politics and project of pedagogy can be constructed to create the conditions for social agency and institutionalized change among postmodern youth.

For many postmodern youth, showing up for adulthood at the fin de siècle means pulling back on hope and trying to put off the future rather than take up the modernist challenge of trying to shape it. Postmodern cultural criticism has captured much of the ennui among youth and has made clear that "what used to be the pessimism of a radical fringe is now the shared assumption of a generation" (Anshaw, 1992, p. 27). Postmodern cultural criticism has helped to alert educators and others to the fault lines marking a generation, regardless of race or class, who seem neither motivated by nostalgia for some lost conservative vision of America nor at home in the new world order paved with the promises of the expanding electronic information highway. For most commentators, youth have become "strange," "alien," and disconnected from the real world.

For instance, in Gus Van Sant's film, *My Own Private Idaho*, the main character, Mike, who hustles his sexual wares for money, is a dreamer lost in fractured memories of a mother who deserted him as a child. Caught between flashbacks of Mom shown in 8-millimeter color and the video world of motley street hustlers and their clients, Mike moves through his existence by falling asleep in times of stress only to awake in different geographic and spatial locations. What holds Mike's psychic and geographic travels together is the metaphor of sleep, the dream of escape, and the ultimate realization that even memories cannot fuel hope for the future. Mike becomes a metaphor for an entire generation forced to sell themselves in a world with no hope, a generation that aspires to nothing, that works at degrading McJobs, and that lives in a world in which chance and randomness rather than struggle, community, and solidarity drive their fate.

A more disturbing picture of youth can be found in *River's Edge*. Teenage anomie and drugged apathy are given painful expression in the depiction of a group of working-class youth who are casually told by John, one of their friends, that he has strangled his girlfriend, another of the group's members, and has left her nude body on the riverbank. The group visit the site at various times to view and probe the dead body of the girl. Seemingly unable to grasp the significance of the event, the youths initially hold off on informing anyone of the murder and with different degrees of concern initially try to protect John, the teenage sociopath, from being caught by the police.

The youths in *River's Edge* drift through a world of broken families, blaring rock music, schooling marked by dead time, and a general indifference to life in general. Decentered and fragmented, they view death like life itself, as merely a spectacle, a matter of style rather than substance. In one sense, these youth share the quality of being "asleep" that is depicted in *My Own Private Idaho*. But what is more disturbing in *River's Edge* is that lost innocence gives way not merely to teenage myopia but to a culture in which human life is experienced as a voyeuristic seduction, a video game, good for passing time and diverting oneself from the pain of the moment. Despair and indifference cancel out the language of ethical discriminations and social responsibility while elevating the immediacy of pleasure to the defining moment of agency.

In *River's Edge*, history as social memory is reassembled through vignettes of 1960s types portrayed as either burned-out bikers or the ex-radical-turned-teacher, whose moralizing relegates politics to simply cheap opportunism. Exchanges among the young people in *River's Edge* appear like projections of a generation waiting either to fall asleep or to commit suicide. After talking about how he murdered his girlfriend, John blurts out, "You do shit, it's done, and then you die." Pleasure, violence, and death, in this case, reassert how a generation of youth takes seriously the dictum that life imitates art or how life is shaped within a violent culture of images in which, as another character states, "it might be easier being dead." To which her boyfriend, a Wayne's World type, replies, "Bullshit! You couldn't get stoned anymore."

River's Edge and *My Own Private Idaho* reveal the seamy and dark side of a youth culture while employing the Hollywood mixture of fascination and horror to titillate the audiences drawn to these films. Employing the postmodern aesthetic of revulsion, locality, randomness,

and senselessness, youth in these films appear to be constructed outside of a broader cultural and economic landscape. Instead, they become visible only through visceral expressions of psychotic behavior
or the brooding experience of a self-imposed comatose alienation.

One of the more celebrated youth films of the 1990s is Richard Link-
later's *Slacker*. A decidedly low-budget film, *Slacker* attempts in both
form and content to capture the sentiments of a twenty-something generation of white youth who reject most of the values of the Reagan/
Bush era but have a difficult time imagining what an alternative might
look like. Distinctly nonlinear in its format, *Slacker* takes place in a
twenty-four-hour time frame in the college town of Austin, Texas. Borrowing its antinarrative structure from films such as Luis Buñuel's
Phantom of Liberty and Max Ophuls's *La Ronde*, *Slacker* is loosely organized around brief episodes in the lives of a variety of characters, none
of whom are connected to each other except that each provides the pre-
text to lead the audience to the next character in the film.

Sweeping through bookstores, coffee shops, auto-parts yard, bed-
rooms, and nightclubs, *Slacker* focuses on a disparate group of young
people who possess little hope in the future and drift from job to job
speaking a hybrid argot of bohemian intensities and new age/pop cult
babble. The film portrays a host of young people who randomly move
from one place to the next, border crossers with no sense of where they
have come from or where they are going. In this world of multiple realities, "schizophrenia emerges as the psychic norm of late capitalism"
(Hebdige, 1988, p. 88). Characters play in bands with such names as
"Ultimate Loser," talk about being forcibly hospitalized by their parents, and one neopunker attempts to sell Madonna's pap smear to two
acquaintances she meets in the street. "Check it out, I know it's kind
of disgusting, but it's like sort of getting down to the real Madonna."

This is a world in which language is wedded to an odd mix of nostalgia, popcorn philosophy, and MTV babble. Talk is organized around
comments like, "I don't know . . . I've traveled . . . and when you get
back you can't tell whether it really happened to you or if you just saw
it on TV." Alienation is driven inward and emerges in comments like
"I feel stuck." Irony slightly overshadows a refusal to imagine any
kind of collective struggle. Reality seems too desperate to care about.
This is humorously captured in one instance by a young man who suggests, "You know how the slogan goes, workers of the world, unite?
We say, workers of the world, relax." People talk but appear disconnected from themselves and each other; lives traverse each other with
no sense of community or connection. There is a pronounced sense in
Slacker of youth caught in the throes of new information technologies

that contain their aspirations while holding out the promise of some sense of agency.

At rare moments in the three films, the political paralysis of solipsistic refusal is offset by instances in which some characters recognize the importance of the image as a vehicle for cultural production, as a representation apparatus that not only can make certain experiences available but can also be used to produce alternative realities and social practices. The power of the image is present in the way the camera follows characters, at once stalking them and confining them to a gaze that is both constraining and incidental. In one scene, a young man appears in a video-filled apartment surrounded by television sets that he claims he has had on for years. He points out that he has invented a game called "A Video Virus," in which through the use of a special technology he can push a button and insert himself onto any of the screens and perform any one of a number of actions. When asked by another character what this is about, he answers, "Well, we all know the psychic powers of the televised image. But we need to capitalize on it and make it work for us instead of working for it."

This theme is taken up in two other scenes. In one short clip, a history graduate student shoots a gun at the video camera he is using to film himself, indicating a self-consciousness about the power of the image and the ability to control it at the same time. In another scene (with which the film concludes), a carload of people, all equipped with Super 8 cameras, drive up to a large hill and throw their cameras into a canyon. The film ends with the images being recorded by the cameras as they cascade to the bottom of the cliff, in what suggests a moment of release and liberation.

Within the postmodern culture depicted in these three films, there are no master narratives at work, no epic modernist dreams, nor is there any element of social agency that accompanies the individualized sense of dropping out, of self-consciously courting chaos and uncertainty.

In many respects, these movies present a slacker culture of white youth who are both terrified and fascinated by the media, who appear overwhelmed by "the danger and wonder of future technologies, the banality of consumption, the thrill of brand names, [and] the difficulty of sex in alienated relationships" (Kopkind, 1992, p. 183). The significance of these films rests, in part, in their attempt to capture the sense of powerlessness that increasingly cuts across race, class, and generations. But what is missing from the films—along with the various books, articles, and reportage concerning what is often called the Nowhere Generation, Generation X, 13thGen, or Slackers—is any sense of the larger political and social conditions in which youth are being framed. What in fact should be seen as a social commentary about "dead-end capitalism" emerges simply as a celebration of refusal dressed up in a rhetoric of aesthetics, style, fashion, and solipsistic protests. Within this type of commentary, postmodern criticism is useful but limited because of its often-theoretical inability to take up the relationship between identity and power, biography and the commodification of everyday life, or the limits of agency in a post-Fordist economy as part of a broader project of possibility linked to issues of history, struggle, and transformation.

The contours of this type of criticism are captured in a comment by Andrew Kopkind, a keen observer of slacker culture:

> The domestic and economic relationships that have created the new consciousness are not likely to improve in the few years left in this century, or in the years of the next, when the young slackers will be middle-agers. The choices for young people will be increasingly constricted. In a few years, a steady job at a mall outlet or a food chain may be all that's left for the majority of college graduates. Life is more and more like a lottery—is a lottery—with nothing but the luck of the draw determining whether you get a recording contract, get your screenplay produced, or get a job with your M.B.A. Slacking is thus a rational response to casino capitalism, the randomization of success, and the utter arbitrariness of power. If no talent is still enough, why bother to hone your skills? If it is impossible to find a good job, why not slack out and enjoy life? (1992, p. 187)

The pedagogical challenge represented by the emergence of a postmodern generation of youth has not been lost on advertisers and market research analysts. According to a 1992 Roper Organization, Inc., study, the current generation of eighteen-to-twenty-nine-year-olds have an annual buying power of $125 billion. Addressing the interests and tastes of this generation, "McDonald's, for instance, has introduced hip-hop music and images to promote burgers and fries, ditto Coca-Cola, with its frenetic commercials touting Coca-Cola Classic" (Hollingsworth, 1993, p. 30). Benetton, Reebok, and other companies have followed suit in their attempts to mobilize the desires, identities, and buying patterns of a new generation of youth. What appears as a dire expression of the postmodern condition to some theorists becomes for others a challenge to invent new market strategies for corporate interests. In this scenario, youth may be experiencing the conditions of postmodernism, but corporate advertisers are attempting to theorize a pedagogy of consumption as part of a new way of appropriating postmodern differences.

What educators need to do is to make the pedagogical more political by addressing both the conditions through which they teach and what it means to learn from a generation that is experiencing life in a way that is vastly different from the representations offered in modernist versions of schooling. The emergence of the electronic media coupled with a diminishing faith in the power of human agency has undermined the traditional visions of schooling and the meaning of pedagogy. The language of lesson plans and upward mobility and the forms of teacher authority on which it was based have been radically delegitimated by the recognition that culture and power are central to the authority–knowledge relationship. Modernism's faith in the past has given way to a future for which traditional markers no longer make sense.

Postmodern Education

Postmodern discourses offer the promise, but not the solution, for alerting educators to a new generation of border youth. Indications of the conditions and characteristics that define such youth are far from uniform or agreed upon. But the daunting fear of essentializing the category of youth should not deter educators and cultural critics from addressing the effects on a current generation of young people, who appear hostage to the vicissitudes of a changing economic order, with its legacy of diminished hopes, on the one hand, and a world of schizoid images, proliferating public spaces, and the increasing fragmentation, uncertainty, and randomness that structure postmodern daily life, on the other.

Central to this issue is whether educators are dealing with a new kind of student forged within organizing principles shaped by the intersection of the electronic image, popular culture, and a dire sense of indeterminacy. Differences aside, the concept of border youth represents less a distinct class, membership, or social group than a referent for naming and understanding the emergence of a set of conditions, translations, border crossings, attitudes, and dystopian sensibilities among youth that cuts across race and class and that represents a fairly new phenomenon.

In this scenario, the experiences of contemporary Western youth in the late-modern world are being ordered around coordinates that structure the experience of everyday life outside of the unified principles and maps of certainty that offered up comfortable and secure representations to previous generations. Youth increasingly rely less on the maps of modernism to construct and affirm their identities; instead, they are faced with the task of finding their way through a decentered cultural landscape no longer caught in the grip of a technology of print, closed narrative structures, or the certitude of a secure economic future. The new emerging technologies that construct and position youth represent interactive terrains that cut across "language and culture, without narrative requirements, without character complexities. . . . Narrative complexity [has given] way to design complexity; story [has given] way to a sensory environment" (Parkes, 1994, p. 50).

A postmodern pedagogy must address the shifting attitudes, representations, and desires of this new generation of youth being produced within the current historical, economic, and cultural juncture. For example, the terms of identity and the production of new maps of meaning must be understood within new hybridized cultural practices inscribed in relations of power that intersect differently with race, class, gender, and sexual orientation. But such differences must be understood not only in terms of the context of their struggles but also through a shared language of resistance that points to hope and possibility. This is where the legacy of a critical modernism becomes valuable: it reminds us of the importance of the language of public life, democratic struggle, and the imperatives of liberty, equality, and justice.

Educators need to understand how different identities among youth are being produced in spheres generally ignored by schools. Included here are an analysis of how pedagogy works to produce, circulate, and confirm particular forms of knowledge and desires in those diverse public and popular spheres in which sounds, images, print, and electronic culture attempt to harness meaning for and against the possibility of expanding social justice and human dignity. Shopping malls, street communities, video halls, coffee shops, television culture, and other elements of popular culture must become serious objects of school knowledge. But more is at stake here than an ethnography of those public spheres in which individual and social identities are constructed and struggled over. More important is the need to fashion a language of ethics and politics that discriminates between relations that do violence and those that promote diverse and democratic public cultures and through which youth and others can understand their problems and concerns as part of a larger effort to interrogate and disrupt the dominant narratives of national identity, economic privilege, and individual empowerment.

Pedagogy must redefine its relationship to modernist forms of culture, privilege, and canonicity and serve as a vehicle of translation and cross-fertilization. Pedagogy as a critical cultural practice needs to open up new institutional spaces in which students can experience and define what it means to be cultural producers capable of both reading different texts and producing them, of moving in and out of theoretical discourses but never losing sight of the need to theorize for themselves. Moreover, if critical educators are to move beyond the postmodern prophets of hyperreality, politics must not be exclusively fashioned to plugging into the new electronically mediated community. The struggle for power is not merely about expanding the range of texts that constitute the politics of representation; it is also about struggling within and against those institutions that wield economic and cultural power.

It is becoming increasingly fashionable to argue for a postmodern pedagogy in which it is important to recognize that "one chief effect of electronic hypertext lies in the way it challenges now conventional assumptions about teachers, learners, and the institutions they inhabit" (Landow, 1992, p. 120). As important as this concern is for refiguring the nature of the relationship between authority and knowledge and the pedagogical conditions necessary for decentering the curriculum and opening up new pedagogical spaces, it does not go far enough and runs the risk of degenerating into another hyped-up, methodological fix.

Postmodern pedagogy must be more sensitive to how teachers and students negotiate both texts and identities, but it must do so through a political project that articulates its own authority within a critical understanding of how the self recognizes others as subjects rather than as objects of history. In other words, postmodern pedagogy must address how power is written on, within, and between different groups as part of a broader effort to reimagine schools as democratic public spheres. Authority in this instance is linked to autocritique and becomes a political and ethical practice through which students become accountable to themselves and others. By making the political project of schooling primary, educators can define and debate the parameters through which communities of difference (defined by relations of representation and reception within overlapping and transnational systems of information, exchange, and distribution) can address what it means to be educated as a practice of empowerment. In this instance, schools can be rethought as public spheres, actively engaged in producing new forms of democratic community organized as sites of translation, negotiation, and resistance.

What is also needed by postmodern educators is a more specific understanding of how affect and ideology mutually construct the knowledge, resistances, and sense of identity that students negotiate as they work through dominant and rupturing narratives attempting in different ways to secure particular forms of authority. Fabienne Worth is right in castigating postmodern educators for undervaluing the problematic nature of the relationship between "desire and the critical enterprise" (Worth, 1993, p. 8). A postmodern pedagogy needs to address how the issue of authority can be linked to democratic processes in the classroom that do not promote pedagogical terrorism and yet still offer representations, histories, and experiences that allow students to critically address the construction of their own subjectivities as they simultaneously engage in an ongoing "process of negotiation between the self and other" (ibid., p. 26).

The conditions and problems of contemporary border youth may be postmodern, but they will have to be engaged through a willingness to interrogate the world of public politics while at the same time recognizing the limits of postmodernism's more useful insights. In part, this means rendering postmodernism more political by appropriating modernity's call for a better world while abandoning its linear narratives of Western history, unified culture, disciplinary order, and technological progress.

In this case, the pedagogical importance of uncertainty and indeterminacy can be rethought through a modernist notion of the dreamworld, in which youth and others can shape, without the benefit of master narratives, the conditions for producing new ways of learning, engaging, and positing the possibilities for social struggle and solidarity. Radical educators cannot subscribe either to an apocalyptic emptiness nor to a politics of refusal that celebrates the immediacy of experience over the more profound dynamic of social memory and moral outrage forged within and against conditions of exploitation, oppression, and the abuse of power. Postmodern pedagogy needs to confront history as more than simulacrum and ethics as something other than the casualty of incommensurable language games. Postmodern educators need to take a stand without standing still, to engage their own politics as public intellectuals without essentializing the ethical referents to address human suffering.

In addition, a postmodern pedagogy needs to go beyond a call for refiguring the curriculum so as to include new information technologies. It needs to assert a politics that makes the relationship among authority, ethics, and power central to a pedagogy that expands rather than closes down the possibilities of a radical democratic society. Within this discourse, images do not dissolve reality into simply another text. On the contrary, representations become central to revealing the structures of power relations at work in the public, schools, society, and the larger global order. Difference does not succumb to fashion in this logic (another touch of ethnicity); instead, difference becomes a marker of struggle in an ongoing movement toward a shared conception of justice and a radicalization of the social order.

Notes

1. Needless to say, one can find a great deal of theoretical material that refuses to dismiss postmodern discourses so easily and in doing so performs a theoretical service in unraveling its progressive from its reactionary tendencies. Early examples can be found in Hal Foster (1985); Hebdige (1988); Vattimo (1992); Ross (1988); Hutcheon (1988); Collins (1989); Connor (1989); Chambers (1990); Aronowitz and Giroux (1991); Best and Kellner (1990); Denzin (1991); Owens (1992).

References

Anderson, Perry. 1984. "Modernity and Revolution." *New Left Review*, no. 144: 96–113.

———. 1998. *The Origins of Postmodernity*. New York: Verso.

Anshaw, Carol. 1992. "Days of Whine and Poses." *Village Voice*, November 10.

Aronowitz, Stanley, and Henry A. Giroux. 1991. *Postmodern Education*. Minneapolis: University of Minnesota Press.

———. 1993. *Education Still under Siege*. 2d ed. Westport: Bergin and Garvey.

Bauman, Zygmunt. 1992. *Intimations of Postmodernity*. New York: Routledge.

Berube, Michael. 1992–93. "Exigencies of Value." *Minnesota Review*, no. 39: 63–87.

Bell, Daniel. 1976. *The Cultural Contradictions of Capitalism*. New York: Basic Books.

Best, Stephen, and Douglas Kellner. 1990. *Postmodern Theory*. New York: Guilford.

Blythe, Scott. 1993. "Generation Xed." *Maclean's*, August.

Bordo, Susan. 1993. *Unbearable Weight: Feminism, Western Culture, and the Body*. Berkeley: University of California Press.

Butler, Judith. 1991. "Contingent Foundations: Feminism and the Question of Postmodernism." In Judith Butler and Joan Scott, eds., *Feminists Theorize the Political*. New York: Routledge.

Chambers, Iain. 1990. *Border Dialogues*. New York: Routledge.

Clarke, John. 1991. *New Times and Old Enemies: Essays on Cultural Studies in America*. New York: Harper Collins.

Collins, Jim. 1989. *Uncommon Cultures*. New York: Routledge.

Connor, Steven. 1989. *Postmodernist Culture*. Cambridge: Basil Blackwell.

Denzin, Norman. 1991. *Images of a Postmodern Society*. Newbury Park, Calif.: Sage.

Docherty, Thomas, ed. 1993. *Postmodernism: A Reader*. New York: Columbia University Press.

Eagleton, Terry. 1985. "Capitalism, Modernism, and Postmodernism." *New Left Review*, no. 185: 60–73.

Ebert, Teresa. 1991. "Writings in the Political: Resistance (Post)modernism." *Legal Studies Forum* 15: 291–303.

Foster, Hal, ed. 1985. *Postmodern Culture*. London: Pluto.

Giroux, Henry. 1988. *Schooling and the Struggle for Public Life*. Minneapolis: University of Minnesota Press.

————. 1991. *Border Crossings*. New York: Routledge.

Habermas, Jürgen. 1978. *The Philosophical Discourse of Modernity*. Cambridge: MIT Press.

Harvey, David. 1989. *The Conditions of Postmodernity*. Cambridge: Basil Blackwell.

Hebdige, Dick. 1988. *Hiding in the Light*. New York: Routledge.

Hollingsworth, Pierce. 1993. "The New Generation Gaps: Graying Boomers, Golden Agers, and Generation X." *Food Technology* 47:30.

Howe, Neil, and Bill Strauss. 1993. *13th Gen: Abort, Retry, Ignore, Fail?* New York: Vantage.

Hunter, Ian. 1988. *Culture and Government: The Emergence of Literary Education*. London: Macmillan.

Hutcheon, Linda. 1988. *The Poetics of Postmodernism*. New York: Routledge.

Jencks, Charles. 1992. "The Postmodern Agenda." In Jencks, ed., *The Postmodern Reader*. New York: St. Martin's.

Jameson, Fredric. 1998. *The Cultural Turn: Selected Writings on the Postmodern: 1983–1998*. New York: Verso.

Jost, Kenneth. 1993. "Downward Mobility." *Congressional Quarterly Researcher* 3:627–44.

Kopkind, Andrew. 1992. "Slacking toward Bethlehem." *Grand Street*, no. 44: 177–88.

Landow, George. 1992. *Hypertext: The Convergence of Contemporary Critical Theory and Technology*. Baltimore: Johns Hopkins University Press, 1992.

Lemert, Charles. 1997. *Postmodernism Is Not What You Think*. Cambridge: Basil Blackwell.

MacCannell, Dean. 1992. *Empty Meeting*. New York: Routledge.

Mercer, Kobena. 1992. " '1968': Periodizing Politics and Identity." In Lawrence Grossberg, Cary Nelson, and Paula Treichler, eds., *Cultural Studies*. New York: Routledge.

Natoli, Joseph, and Linda Hutcheon, eds. 1993. *A Postmodern Reader*. Albany: SUNY Press.

Owens, Craig. 1992. *Beyond Recognition: Representation, Power, and Culture: Craig Owens*. Ed. Scott Bryson et. al. Berkeley: University of California Press.

Parkes, Walter. 1994. "Random Access, Remote Control: The Evolution of Story Telling." *Omni*, January.

Patton, Paul. 1988. "Giving up the Ghost: Postmodernism and Anti-Nihilism." In Lawrence Grossberg, ed. *It's a Sin*. Sydney: Power.

Ross, Andrew, ed. 1988. *Universal Abandon? The Politics of Postmodernism*. Minneapolis: University of Minnesota Press.

Tomlinson, John. 1991. *Cultural Imperialism*. Baltimore: Johns Hopkins University Press.

Vattimo, Gianni. 1992. *The Transparent Society*. Baltimore: Johns Hopkins University Press.

Virilio, Paul. 1991. *Lost Dimension.* Trans. Daniel Moshenberg. New York: Semiotext(e).

Worth, Fabienne. 1993. "Postmodern Pedagogy in the Multicultural Classroom: For Inappropriate Teachers and Imperfect Strangers." *Cultural Critique,* no. 25 (Fall): 5–32.

5

Our Common Culture:
A Poisonous Pedagogy

Donaldo Macedo

Reporter: Mr. Ghandi, what do you think of modern civilization?

Ghandi: That would be a good idea.

What All Americans Need to Know

In his celebrated book *Dictionary of Cultural Literacy: What All Americans Need to Know*, E. D. Hirsch and colleagues provide a pointed attack on American education that, for too long, has reduced learning to skills acquisition devoid of cultural content (Hirsch, Kett, and Tuefil, 1988). As an alternative, Hirsch argues that schools should deemphasize "process" and reemphasize "content," which is, in his view, rooted in our "common cultural" background knowledge. What Hirsch fails to recognize is that his treatment of culture is "descriptive rather than anthropological and political. . . . Its meaning is fixed in the past, and its essence is that it provides the public with a common referent for communication and exchange" (Aronowitz and Giroux, 1988, p. 185).

However, Hirsch's common cultural shared information is nothing less and nothing more than a veiled cultural information-banking model based on a selective selection of Western cultural features that "dismisses the notion that culture has any determinate relation to the practices of power and politics or is largely defined as a part of an ongoing struggle to move history, experience, knowledge, and the meaning of everyday life in one's terms" (Aronowitz and Giroux, 1988, p. 186).

What is more pernicious than Hirsch's fossilized encyclopedia of "our common cultural" background knowledge is his selective omis-

117

sion of cultural facts that all Americans also need to know but are prevented from knowing. This is part of the ongoing "poisonous pedagogy" designed "to impart . . . from the beginning false information and beliefs that have been passed on from generation to generation and dutifully accepted by the young even though they are not only unproved but are demonstrably false" (Miller, 1990, p. 54). According to Alice Miller, to ensure that the received belief and value system is continually reproduced, the recipients "shall never be aware for their own good" of the mechanisms inherent in "poisonous pedagogy," which involve "laying traps, lying, duplicity, subterfuge, manipulation, 'scare' tactics, withdrawal of love, isolation, distrust, humiliation . . . scorn, ridicule, and coercion even to the point of torture" (ibid.).

Although Alice Miller's work focuses mostly on child-rearing practices, the mechanisms of poisonous pedagogy also inform our education and even our government. We do not have to look further than our newspaper headlines to identify explicit mechanisms of poisonous pedagogy in the behavior of our politicians. For instance, in an investigation of corrupt politicians in the Massachusetts legislature, the *Boston Globe* (May 27, 1993) concluded that "the Beacon Hill system often seems designed to obfuscate the truth, hinder public scrutiny and conceal the identity of special interests and their agents." The prevalent lying and concealment of truth are part and parcel of our political culture and are best measured by the public's resignation to such lies.

Anyone who followed the Iran–contra investigation can attest that Presidents Reagan and Bush were less than truthful to the public, and they were no less deceitful about U.S. complicity in concealing the truth about the carnage and crimes against humanity committed by the El Salvadoran army in the massacre of El Mozote in 1981, the vicious murders of six Jesuit priests, and the rape and murder of four American churchwomen. Yet, public resignation to such lies is so complete that there was little uproar when the *Boston Globe* (March 18, 1993) headlined, "The Truth Comes on a Dirty US War." The same public resignation to lies and deceit by our public officials was evident when President Bush pardoned Caspar Weinberger, who was accused of lying to Congress in the Iran–contra affair. The same public resignation allows the former secretary of state, Alexander M. Haig Jr., to not be accountable for his irresponsible assertion that the four churchwomen raped and murdered by the El Salvadoran army in 1980 may have been killed as they tried to run a roadblock.

The mechanisms of poisonous pedagogy are also part and parcel of our educational system, which is designed to instill obedience so as to require students to "1) willingly do as they are told, 2) willingly refrain from doing what is forbidden, and 3) accept the rules for their sake"

(Miller, 1990, p. 13). Thus, obedience becomes a pivotal tool for the reproduction of the dominant culture to the extent that independent thoughts and actions are regulated by the system or repressed by the individual, who has submitted his or her will to the entrapment of poisonous pedagogy. The rule of obedience in eradicating critical thought and independent action was well understood throughout history:

> Obedience is so important that all education is actually nothing other than learning how to obey. It is a generally recognized principle that persons of high estate who are destined to rule whole nations must learn the art of governance by way of first learning obedience. *Qui nescit obedire, nescit imperare*: the reason for this is that obedience teaches a person to be zealous in observing the law, which is the first quality of a ruler. Thus, after one has driven out willfulness as a result of one's first labors with children, the chief goal of one's further labors must be obedience. (Miller, 1990, pp. 12–13)

Obedience, however is not easily instilled in individuals. It requires a sophisticated implementation of the ingredients of poisonous pedagogy, which include the use of scare tactics, lies, manipulation, and other means designed to get individuals to submit to the rule of law and to accept what has been presented as sacred. All this must take place in a carefully crafted manner so that the individual "won't notice and will therefore not be able" to expose the lies. Hitler was fully aware of this fact: "It also gives us a very special, secret pleasure to see how unaware the people around us are of what is really happening to them" (quoted in Miller, 1990, p. 63). I would argue that many of our own educators and politicians enjoy a "very special special, secret pleasure" in viewing how anesthetized we have become and how unaware we are of what is really happening to us.

Obedience imposed through lies is accomplished not only through received but false cultural information but also through the omission of cultural facts, such as the horrendous crimes that the Western heritage committed against humanity in order to prevent the possibility of keeping dangerous memories alive. It is, then, not accidental that Hirsch's "shopping mall" (Gannaway, 1994) cultural literacy gives rise to a type of education based on the accumulation of selected cultural facts that are disconnected from the sociocultural world that generated these facts in the first place. Educators who adhere to Hirsch's perspective often contribute to the fragmentation of knowledge due to their reductionist view of the act of knowing. The acquisition of what all Americans need to know in a fossilized encyclopedic manner prevents the learner from relating the flux of information so as to gain a critical reading of the world. This implies, obviously, the ability of learners to critically understand how Hirsch's view of "widely accepted cultural values" often equates Western culture with civilization, while leaving unnoted Western culture's role in "civilizing" the "primitive others."

To execute its civilizing tasks, Western culture resorted to barbarism so as to save the "other" cultural subjects from their primitive selves. Ironically, Hirsch neglects to include in his dictionary information that would show how Western culture, in the name of civilization and religion, subjugated, enslaved, and plundered Africa, Asia, and the Americas. If this perspective of cultural literacy allowed readers to become critical, encouraging them to apply rigorous standards of science, intellectual honesty, and academic truth in their inquiry, they would arrive at a much more complex response than is allowed for in the prevailing version of our cultural literacy.

Critical readers would also question why the dictionary fails to inform American readers that "Indian towns and villages were attacked and burned, their inhabitants murdered or sold into foreign slavery" (Zinn, 1990, p. 25). These often-omitted historical facts were described by William Bradford, the governor of Plymouth Colony: "It was a fearful sight to see [the Indians] thus frying in the fire and the streams of blood quenching the same, and horrible was the stink and scent thereof; but the victory seemed a sweet sacrifice, and [the settlers] gave the praise thereof to God, who had wrought so wonderfully for them" (Stannard, 1992, p. 430). Critical readers would also question why Hirsch's cultural literacy conveniently fails to discuss how history shows us convincingly and factually that the United States systematically violated the Pledge of Allegiance from the legalization of slavery, the denial of women's rights, the near-genocide of Indians, to the contemporary discriminatory practices against people who, by virtue of their race, ethnicity, class, or gender, are not treated with the dignity and respect called for in the pledge. If Hirsch, Arthur Schlesinger, Jr., and others did not suffer from historical amnesia, they would include in our common cultural literacy the following observation:

If you were a colonist, you knew that your technology was superior to the Indians'. You knew that you were civilized, and they were savages. . . . But your superior technology proved insufficient to extract anything. The Indians, keeping to themselves, laughed at your superior methods and lived from the land more abundantly and with less labor than you did. . . . And when your own people started deserting in order to live with them, it was too much. . . . So you killed the Indians, tortured them, burned their villages, burned their corn fields. It proved your superiority, in spite of your failures. And you gave similar treatment to any of your own people who succumbed to their savage ways of life. But you still did not grow much corn. (Zinn, 1990, p. 184)

One can now begin to see why Hirsch's information-banking model of cultural literacy is based on a selective form of history. His omission of important historical facts in his common cultural list that every American needs to know points to the ideological nature of his pedagogy and constitutes the foundation for what I call the pedagogy of big lies. If we were to compare and juxtapose Hirsch's texts with the historical information he leaves out of his cultural inventory list, we would begin to understand the importance of keeping readers from knowing the truth for their own good. The left column below is taken from the *Dictionary of Cultural Literacy: What Every American Needs to Know* (Hirsch, Kett, and Tuefil, 1988). The column on the right elaborates historical facts to fill the gap of what is omitted from the dictionary.

What every American needs to know

Government of the people, by the people, and for the people: Words from the Gettysburg Address of Abraham Lincoln, often quoted as a definition of democracy.

What every American needs to know but is prevented from knowing

These words were not meant for African Americans, since Abraham Lincoln also once declared: "I will say, then, that I am not, nor ever have been in favor of ringing about in any way the social and political equality of white and black races. . . . I as much as any other man am in favor of having the superior position assigned to the white race" (Zinn, 1990, p. 184).

Indentured servant: A person under contract to work for another person for a definite period of time, usually without pay but in exchange for free passage to a new country. During the seventeenth century most of the white laborers in Maryland and Virginia came from England as indentured servants.

Slavery: Although omitted from Hirsch's cultural list, slavery involved kidnapping Africans, breaking up families, and shipping Africans to the Americas to be sold to white masters to perform forced labor under duress and inhuman conditions, often involving undignified and denigrating jobs. Slavery was legal and protected by U.S. laws until the Emancipation Proclamation, even though slavery continued unabated long after the Emancipation Proclamation.

Give me liberty or give me death: Words from a speech by Patrick

Patrick Henry's words were not meant for African slaves or American

Henry urging the American colonies to revolt against England. Henry spoke only a few weeks before the Revolutionary War began: "Gentlemen may cry peace, peace, but there is no peace. The war is actually begun. The next gale that sweeps from the north will ring to our ears the clash of resounding arms. Our brethren are already in the field. . . . Is life so dear, or peace so sweet, as to be purchased at the price of chains and slavery? Forbid it, Almighty God! I know not what course others may take, but for me, give me liberty or give me death!"

Indians. African Americans and American Indians continued throughout the history of the United States to experience subjugation, leading Malcolm X to pronounce in 1964 the following: "No, I'm not an American. I'm one of the 22 million black people who are the victims of Americanism. . . . One of the . . . victims of democracy, nothing but disguised hypocrisy. So, I'm not standing here speaking to you as an American, or a patriot, or a flag-saluter, or a flag-waver—no, not I! I'm speaking as a victim of this American system. And I see America through the eyes of the victim. I don't see any American dream; I see an American nightmare!" (Zinn, 1990, p. 65).

Navahos: A tribe of Native Americans, the most numerous in the United States. The Navahos have reservations in the Southwest. The Navahos were forced to move by United States troops under Kit Carson in 1864. They call the march, on which many died, the Long Walk. Today, they are known for their houses, called hogans, made of logs and earth; for their work as ranchers and shepherds; and for their skill in producing blankets and turquoise and silver jewelry.

"The United States is founded on the destruction of the native population. Before Columbus the population north of the Rio Grande was maybe 12–15 million. At the turn of the century it was 200,000. The whole history of the conquest of the continent from the time that the saintly Pilgrims landed is the destruction of the native population by various means, sometimes just plain mass slaughter, like the Pequot Massacre by the Puritans or George Washington's destruction of the Iroquois civilization right in the middle of the War of Independence, and many later events running through the conquest of the national territory. Sometimes it was criminal expulsion like Jackson's expulsion of the Cherokees, really hard-line things. Anyway, that's the history" (Chomsky, 1988, pp. 683–84).

Plymouth Rock: The rock, in what is now Plymouth, Massachusetts, near which the Mayflower, carrying the Pilgrims, landed in 1620.

Plymouth rock seen through the eyes of American Indians represents the beginning of a quasi-genocide legalized by the Massachusetts legislature, which promulgated a law that provided monetary rewards for dead Indians. "For every scalp or male Indian brought in . . . forty pounds. For every scalp of such female Indian or male Indian under the age of twelve years that shall be killed . . . twenty pounds" (Zinn, 1990, pp. 234–35).

Big Stick Diplomacy: International negotiations backed by the threat of force. The phrase comes from a proverb quoted by Theodore Roosevelt, who said that the United States should "speak softly and carry a big stick."

Big-stick diplomacy characterizes U.S. foreign policy, particularly in Latin America. Recent examples of such diplomacy are the U.S. invasion of Grenada under Ronald Reagan, the U.S. bombing of Libya under Ronald Reagan, the U.S. invasion of Nicaragua via a proxy, the contras, under Ronald Reagan, and the U.S. invasion of Panama under George Bush.

Japanese-Americans, internment: An action taken by the federal government in 1942, after the air force of Japan bombed Pearl Harbor and brought the United States into World War II. Government officials feared that Americans of Japanese descent living on the west coast might cooperate in an invasion of the United States by Japan. Accordingly, over 100,000 of these residents were sent into relocation camps inland, many losing their homes and jobs in the process. About two-thirds of those moved were U.S. citizens. (See Nisei.) Many Japanese-Americans, including an entire army battalion, distinguished themselves in combat in World War II.

"To the Japanese who lived on the West Coast of the United States, it quickly became clear that the war against Hitler was not accompanied by a spirit of racial equality. . . . One congressman said, 'I am for catching every Japanese in America, Alaska, and Hawaii now and putting them in concentration camps. . . . Damn them! Let's get rid of them now!' Roosevelt, persuaded by racists in the military that the Japanese on the West Coast constituted a threat to the security of the country, signed Executive Order 9066 in February 1942. This empowered the army, without warrants or indictments or hearings, to arrest every Japanese-American on the West Coast—11,000 men, women, and children—to take them from their homes, to transport them to camps far in the interior, and to keep them there under prison conditions. . . . Data uncovered in the 1980s by legal historian Peter Irons showed that the army falsified material in its brief to the Supreme Court. . . . The American press often helped to feed racism. *Time* magazine said, 'The ordinary unreasoning Jap is ignorant. Perhaps he is human. Nothing indicates it.'

"Ota was born in the United States. He remembered what happened in the war: 'On the evening of December 7, 1941, my father was at a wedding. He was dressed in a tuxedo. When the reception was over, the FBI agents were waiting. They rounded up at least a dozen wedding guests and took 'em to county jail. For a few days we didn't know what happened. We heard nothing. When we found out, my mother, my sister went to jail. . . . When my father walked through the door my mother was so humiliated . . . she cried. He was in prisoner's clothing, with a denim jacket and a number on the back. The shame and humiliation just broke her down. . . . Right after that day she got very ill and contracted tuberculosis. She had to be sent to a sanitarium. . . . She was there till she died. My father was transferred to Missoula, Montana. We got letters from him—censored, of course. . . . It was just my sister and myself. I was fifteen, she was twelve. School in camp was a joke. . . . *One of our basis subjects was American history. They talked all the time'* " (Zinn, 1990, 89–90, emphasis mine).

Remember the Alamo: A battle cry in the Texans' struggle for independence from Mexico, later used by Americans in the Mexican wars. It recalled the desperate flight of the Texas defenders of the Alamo, a besieged fort, where they died to the last man.

What is important to note is that the United States, in its history of expansionism and conquest, instigated a war with Mexico so as to later claim half of Mexico's land.

Malcolm X: A political leader of the twentieth century. Malcolm X, a prominent Black Muslim, who explained the group's viewpoint in *The Autobiography of Malcolm X,* was assassinated in 1965.

"The Trap of 'Racism': There are traps that he creates. If you speak in an angry way about what has happened to our people and what is happening to our people, what does he call it? Emotionalism. Pick up on that.

Here the man has got a rope around his neck and because he screams, you know, the cracker that's putting the rope around his neck accuses him of being emotional. You're supposed to have the rope around your neck and holler politely, you know. You're supposed to watch your diction, not shout and make other people—this is how you're supposed to holler. You're supposed to be respectable and responsible when you holler against what they are doing to you" (Malcolm X, speech given on January 24, 1965).

Parks, Rosa: A black seamstress from Montgomery, Alabama, who, in 1965, refused to give up her seat to a white person, as she was legally required to do. Her mistreatment after refusing to give up her seat led to a boycott of the Montgomery buses by supporters of equal rights for black people. This incident was the first major confrontation in the Civil Rights Movement.

Rosa Parks was not just mistreated. She was arrested and placed in jail. According to her, "Well, in the first place, I had been working all day on the job. I was quite tired after spending a full day working. I handled and worked on clothing that white people wear. That didn't come in my mind, but this is what I wanted to know: When and how would one even determine our rights as human beings? . . . It just happened that the driver made a demand and I just didn't feel like obeying his demand. He called a policeman and I was arrested and placed in jail."

Manhattan Project: The code name for the effort to develop atomic bombs for the United States during World War II. The first controlled nuclear reaction took place in Chicago in 1942, and by 1945, bombs had been manufactured that used this chain reaction to produce greater explosive force. The project was carried out in enormous secrecy. After a test explosion in July 1945, the United States dropped atomic bombs on the Japanese cities of Hiroshima and Nagasaki.

Although American intelligence had broken the Japanese code indicating the Japanese readiness to surrender, it did not prevent President Truman from going ahead and, perhaps unnecessarily, bombing two highly populated Japanese cities. Truman said that " 'the world will note that the first atomic bomb was dropped on Hiroshima, a military base. That was because we wished in this first attack to avoid, insofar as possible, the killing of civilians.' It was a preposterous statement. Those 100,000 killed in Hiroshima were almost all civilians. The U.S. Strategic Bombing Survey said in its official report: 'Hiroshima and Nagasaki were chosen as targets because of their concentration of activities and population.' The dropping of the second bomb on Nagasaki seems to have been scheduled in advance, and no one has ever been able to explain why it was dropped. Was it because this was a plutonium bomb whereas the Hiroshima bomb was a uranium bomb? Were the dead and irradiated of Nagasaki victims of a scientific experiment?" (Zinn, 1990, p. 415).

Vietnam War: A war in Southeast Asia, in which the United States fought in the 1960s and 1970s. The war was waged from 1954 to 1975 between communist North Vietnam and noncommunist South Vietnam, two parts of what was once the French colony of Indochina. Vietnamese communists attempted to take over the South, both by invasion from the North and by guerrilla warfare conducted within the South by Viet Cong. Presidents Dwight D. Eisenhower and John F. Kennedy sent increasing numbers of American military advisors to South Vietnam in the late 1950s and early 1960s. Kennedy's successor, President Lyndon Johnson, increased American military support greatly, until half a million United States soldiers were in Vietnam.

American goals in Vietnam proved difficult to achieve, and the communists' Tet Offensive was a severe setback. Report of atrocities committed by both sides in the war disturbed many Americans (see My Lai Massacre). Eventually, President Richard Nixon decreased American troop strength, and sent his secretary of state, Henry Kissinger, to negotiate a cease-fire with

"The need to 'stop communism' was used to justify the invasion of Vietnam and to carry on there a full-scale war in which over a million people died. It was used to justify the bombing of peasant villages, the chemical poisoning of crops, the 'search and destroy missions,' the laying waste of an entire country. GI Charles Hutto, who participated in the massacre of Vietnamese peasants at My Lai, told army investigators: 'I remember the unit's combat assault on My Lai. The night before the mission we had a briefing by Captain Medina. He said everything in the village was communist. So we shot men, women, and children' " (Zinn, 1990, p. 267).

President John F. Kennedy, who considered Vietnam "an important piece of real estate," committed "U.S. planes and U.S. pilots to undertake direct participation, not just control, in the bombing and defoliation operations in South Vietnam directed against the rural population, which was the large majority, about 80% of the population. . . . Adlai Stevenson, our UN ambassador at the time, referred to an 'internal aggression,'

North Vietnam. American troops were withdrawn in 1973, and South Vietnam was completely taken over by communist forces in 1975.

The involvement of the United States in the war was extremely controversial. Some supported wholeheartedly; others opposed it in mass demonstrations and by refusing to serve in the American armed forces (see Draft). Still others seemed to rely on the government to decide the best course of action (see Silent Majority). A large memorial (see Vietnam Memorial) bearing the names of all members of the United States armed services who died in the Vietnam War is in Washington, D.C.

namely the aggression of the Vietnamese, and particularly the Vietnamese peasants, against the United States in South Vietnam. A society that can use phrases such as 'internal aggression' and can perceive the bombing of peasant villages as a defense of either us or our clients, that society has gone a long towards a kind of operative totalitarianism" (Chomsky, 1988, p. 701).

A large black marble memorial contains the names of over 50,000 Americans who perished in the Vietnam War.

Banana republics: A term describing any of several small nations in Latin America that have economies based on a few agricultural crops. The term "banana republic" is often used in a disparaging sense; it suggests an unstable government.

As a term, *banana republic* also refers to the puppet governments installed by the CIA to protect U.S. interests while the vast majority of the population live in dire poverty. The United States often installs and supports dictatorships, giving rise to political instability and periodic civil wars. What follows is a partial list of U.S. invasions of these so-called banana republics to protect the interests of U.S. companies:

• 1854, Nicaragua: U.S. invasion to avenge an insult to the American minister to Nicaragua.

• 1855, Uruguay: Landing of U.S. and European naval forces to protect American interests during an attempted revolution in Montevideo.

• 1954, Guatemala: A legally elected government overthrown by invasion forces of mercenaries trained by the CIA. The government that the United States overthrew was the most democratic Guatemala had ever had. "What was most unsettling to American business interests was that Arbenz [the deposed president] had expropriated 234,000 acres of land owned by United Fruit, offering compensation that United Fruit called 'unacceptable' " (Zinn, 1990, pp. 430–31).

Colonialism: The control of one nation by transplanted people of another nation—often a geographically distant nation that has a different culture and dominant racial or ethnic group (see Ethnicity). A classic example of colonialism is the control of India by Britain from the eighteenth century to 1947. Control that is economic and cultural, rather than political, is often called Neocolonialism.

Although the United States fought for its independence against Britain, it ended up assuming the colonial role in the world, seizing Cuba and Puerto Rico in 1898, the Canal Zone in Panama in 1903, and Hawaii in 1903, and fighting a brutal war to subjugate the Philippines. The United States functions as a de facto neocolonialist power due to its economic and cultural control of Puerto Rico and many Latin American nations. The United States almost always sided with the colonizers in Africa when African countries began their independence wars.

Disenfranchisement: Removal of the franchise, or right to vote.

The disenfranchised often refers to the oppressed "minority" groups in the United States. The dominant group in the United States prefers the term *disenfranchised groups* over *oppressed groups.* With the verb *disenfranchise,* one can never identify the subject, whereas *oppressed* acknowledges an oppressor.

Oligarchy: A system of government in which power is held by a small group.

A classic example of oligarchy is El Salvador, supported by the United States in a civil war that has cost that country 70,000 lives. The United States has spent billions of dollars maintaining a de facto oligarchy in El Salvador while ignoring outrageous human rights violations by the ultra right and military death squads that were responsible for thousands of killings, including the massacre of six Jesuit priests.

Refugees: People who flee a nation, often to escape punishment for their political affiliations or for political dissent.

The United States adopts a double standard toward refugees. It welcomed anti-Sandinista refugees while deporting El Salvadorans who tried to escape political persecution. It welcomes Cuban refugees while it deports Haitian boat people.

Third World: The nonaligned nations—which are often developing nations—of Africa, Asia, and Latin America. They are in a "third" group of nations since they are allied with neither the United States nor the Soviet Union.

Third World also refers to underdeveloped nations. The term is misleading to the extent that we have Third World contexts in First World nations, such as ghettoes, and First World realities in Third World countries.

World Court: A division of the United Nations that settles legal disputes submitted to it by member nations. The International Court of Justice, also called the World Court, meets in The Hague, Netherlands.

Although the World Court mediates legal disputes among nations, it has no power of execution. A classic example of its lack of execution power involves the mining of the Nicaraguan harbor by the United States. The World Court ruled in favor of Nicaragua, but the United States arrogantly dismissed the ruling.

Class: A group of people sharing the same social, economic, or occupational status. The term *class* usually implies a social and economic hierarchy, in which those of higher class standing have greater status, privilege, prestige, and authority. Western societies have traditionally been divided into classes: the upper class or leisure class, the middle class (bourgeoisie), and the lower or working class. For Marxists, the significant classes are the bourgeoisie and the proletariat.

The ruling elite aided by the intelligentsia goes to great lengths to create mechanisms designed to perpetuate the myth that the United States is a classless society. That is why George Bush, during the 1988 presidential campaign, berated his democratic opponent by saying: "I am not going to let that liberal Governor divide this nation. . . . I think that's for European democracies or something else. It isn't for the United States of America. We're not going to be divided by class. . . . We are the land of big dreams, of big opportunities, of fair play, and this attempt to divide America by class is going to fail because the American people realize that we are a very special country, for anybody given the opportunity can make it and fulfill the American dream" (*New York Times,* October 30, 1988). This is the same George Bush who fought for a capital gains tax cut for the rich while threatening to veto a tax cut for the middle class and who put into place severe cuts designed to dismantle social services, including education, for the poor. It is the same George Bush who used the benefit of the capital gains tax to buy his Maine two-million-dollar estate, arguing that his purchase "put money in the pockets of real estate agents and contractors," thus creating jobs. George Bush would be hard put to convince residents of East L.A., Harlem, and East St. Louis that the purchase of his two-million-dollar estate through tax cuts for the rich made their poverty-class conditions any better. In fact, George Bush, while discouraging class struggle debate, was a principle actor in the creation of the biggest gulf between the upper class and the lower class.

According to the U.S. Census Bureau, as analyzed by the Center on Budget and Policy Priorities, "in 1988, the richest fifth of American families received 44 percent of the nation's total family income. That's the highest percentage ever recorded for that segment of the population. On the other hand, the poorest fifth received only 4.6 percent. That's the lowest since 1954. The second-poorest fifth and the middle fifth each received the lowest ever recorded share of the nation's income." The Center on Budget and Policy Priorities says that "while the average income for the bottom 20 percent of households fell in the 1980s, income for the top 1 percent, after taxes, rose 122 percent, from $203,000 to $451,000. The average salary of a person worth over $1 million rose from $515,499 to $770,587. The average wage of a person who earns under $20,000 rose a mere $123, from $8,528 to $8,651."

In the face of glaring evidence of class stratification, politicians and educators in the United States continue to promote the myth that the United States is a classless society. However, it would be hard to convince students in East St. Louis Senior High School that they enjoy class equity in this great land of ours: "East St. Louis Senior High School was awash in sewage for the second time this year. The school had to be shut became of fumes and backed-up toilets. Sewage flowed into the basement, through the floor, then up into the kitchen and the students' bathrooms. The backup, we read, 'occurred in the food preparation areas' " (Kozol, 1991, p. 23).

Declaration of Independence: The fundamental document establishing the United States as a nation, adopted on July 4, 1776. The declaration was ordered and approved by the Continental Congress, and written largely by Thomas Jefferson. It declared the Thirteen Colonies represented in the Continental Congress independent from Great Britain, offered reasons for separation, and laid out the principles for which the Revolutionary War was fought. The signers included John Adams, Benjamin Franklin, John Hancock, and Jefferson. The declaration begins (capitalization and punctuation are modernized):

"When, in the course of human events, it becomes necessary for one people to dissolve the political bands which have connected them with one another, and to assume, among the powers of the earth, the separate and equal station to which the laws of nature and of nature's God entitle them, a decent respect for the opinions of mankind requires that they should declare the causes which impel them to the separation.

"We hold these truths to be self-evident: that all men are created equal; that they are endowed by their cre-

The Declaration of Independence was not meant for the slaves that Thomas Jefferson owned. This is why Frederick Douglass, a well-known abolitionist who, evidently is not included in Hirsch's cultural list, gave the following speech on the Fourth of July, 1852:

"Fellow Citizens. Pardon me, and allow me to ask, why am I called upon to speak here today? Why have I or those I represent to do with your national independence? Are the great principles of political freedom and material justice, embodied in that Declaration of Independence, extended to us? And am I, therefore, called upon to bring our humble offering to the national altar, and to confess the benefits, and to express devout gratitude for the blessings resulting from your independence to us?

"What to the American slave is your Fourth of July? I answer, a day that reveals to him more than all other days of the year the gross injustice and cruelty to which he is the constant victim. To him your celebration is a sham; your boasted liberty an unholy license; your national greatness, swelling vanity; your sounds of

ator with certain unalienable rights; that among these are life, liberty, and the pursuit of happiness; that, to secure these rights, governments are instituted among men, deriving their powers from the consent of the governed; that whenever any form of government becomes destructive of these ends, it is the right of the people to alter or to abolish it, and to institute one government, laying its foundations on such principles, and analyzing its powers in such forms as to them shall seem most likely to effect their safety and happiness."

The day of the adoption of the Declaration of Independence is now commemorated as the Fourth of July, or Independence Day.

rejoicing are empty and heartless; your denunciation of tyrants, brass-fronted impotence; your shouts of liberty and equality, hollow mockery; your prayers and hymns, your sermons and thanks-givings, with all your religious parade and solemnity, are to him more bombast, fraud, deception, impiety, and hypocrisy—with a thin veil to cover up which would disgrace a nation of savages. There is no nation of the earth guilty of practices more shocking and bloody than are the people of these United States at this very hour. Go where you may, search where you will, roam through all the monarchies and despotisms of the Old World, travel through South America, search out every abuse and when you have found the last, lay your facts by the side of the everyday practices of this nation, and you will say with me that, for revolting barbarity and shameless hypocrisy, America reigns without a rival" (Zinn, 1990, p. 178).

The juxtaposition of the texts above points to a pedagogy that enables readers to link the flux of information in order to gain a more critical reading of reality. Instead of just consuming Hirsch's cultural list as facts, readers can rely on other points of reference so as to be able to think more critically, thus recognizing the falsehoods embedded in the various pedagogies created by the dominant class. By and large, dominant education utilizes poisonous pedagogy mechanisms to undermine independent thought, a prerequisite for the "manufacture of consent." It is only through a pedagogy that manufactures consent that a society tolerates gross distortion of realities and the rewriting of history as exemplified in *The History of the United States,* by Robert J. Fields, which is used as a social sciences text in some of Boston's public schools:

> Vietnam is a small country near China. It is thousands of miles from the United States. Vietnam is on the other "side" of the world. But, in the 1960's, it hurt our country badly. . . . The Vietnamese people fought for their freedom. Communists took advantage of the fight. Communists

wanted to make Vietnam a communist country. The people of Vietnam just wanted freedom. . . . The North Vietnam army fought a secret war. They hid and ambushed the Americans. Women and children helped fight against the Americans. . . . Thousands of American soldiers died in Vietnam. Many Americans were against the war. (Fields, 1987, p. 135)

What the above text clearly demonstrates is how history is distorted not only by the presentation of false information but also by the omission of important facts that serve as a counterpoint of reference. For example, in the rewriting of the Vietnam War, Fields fails to account for the over one million Vietnamese who died in the war, not to mention the systematic killing of the elderly, women, and children, as evidenced in the My Lai massacre. Similar massacres were routine, as recalled by Sergeant James Daley: " 'When you come into an enemy village,' we were told [by training instructors in the United States], 'you come in opening fire. You kill everything that's living—women, children, and animals' " (Gibson, 1988, p. 146). Daley's account proves that the My Lai massacre was not an isolated incident. In fact, Shad Meshad, a psychologist who served in Vietnam, describes what he heard from soldiers: "They'd been on sweeps of villages, with orders to leaving nothing living, not even chickens and [water] buffaloes. Well, what the fuck did that mean, following orders like that? Wasn't it Lieutenant Calley who created the stir in the first place? They were doing a Calley every day" (Gibson, 1988, p. 158).

The barbarism of our Western heritage civilization training proved to be lethal for the Vietnamese. Jeffrey Whitmore, a marine, describes another graphic slaughter:

I just happened to be standing alongside the officer when the radioman said, "Look, Sir, we got children rounded up. What do you want us to do with them?" The guy says, "Goddamn it, Marine, you know what to do with them: kill the bastards. If you ain't got the goddamn balls to kill them, Marine, I'll come down and kill the mother-fuckers myself." The Marine said, "Yes, Sir" and hung up the phone. About two or three minutes later I heard babies crying. I heard children crying their fucking lungs out. (Gibson, 1988, p. 147)

Although the vicious acts of violence perpetuated against innocent Vietnamese women and children by our GIs are documented, no history books in school expose students to our crimes against humanity. Thus, it is not surprising that cultural legionnaires such as Hirsch choose to selectively monumentalize certain aspects of our Western heritage while neglecting to report on heinous crimes that Western civilization has committed throughout its history. A more honest account of our Western cultural heritage would not only monumentalize the great deeds in museums and great books but also look at Western civilization through a magnifying mirror so we could see the grotesque and barbaric images of the Western cultural heritage. In other words, historical truth and academic and intellectual honesty would demand that for each museum of fine arts we build in a given city, we should also build a museum of slavery, with graphic accounts of the dehumanization of African Americans, when entire families were split and sold to the highest bidder on the block, and with pictures of lynchings. For each museum of science built in a given city, we should also build a museum of the quasi-genocide of American Indians, their enslavement and the raping, and the expropriation of their land. We should also build a Vietnam museum alongside the Vietnam Veterans Memorial, in which graphic accounts of rape and killing of Vietnamese women by Western heritage trained GI's would be described:

> The girls were unconscious at that point [after repeated rapes]. When they finished raping them, three of the GIs took hand flares and shoved them in the girl's vaginas. . . . No one to hold them down any longer. The girls were bleeding from their mouths, noses, faces, and vaginas. Then they struck the exterior portion of the flares and they exploded inside the girls. Their stomachs started bloating up, and then they exploded. The stomachs exploded, and their intestines were just hanging out of their bodies. (Gibson, 1988, pp. 202–3)

Although I had read a great deal about American GI atrocities in Vietnam, I was revulsed when reading the above, and I immediately called a friend of mine who served in Vietnam to certify if, in fact, such crimes had occurred. My friend, Herman Garcia, who is now a professor at the University of New Mexico at Las Cruces, recounted his experience in Vietnam in the following note:

> The war in Vietnam would be better characterized as "An Account of the Millions of Isolated Incidents of American-Committed Atrocities of the War." As a Chicano and a member of an oppressed cultural and linguistic minority group in the United States, I had no political or ideological knowledge of my role in the war at the age of 19, although I intuitively knew something felt wrong. I just never had a language for expressing the feelings and intuitions I carried.
>   One of the most vivid and horrendous accounts that I have had to live with all these years was the day a soldier in my infantry unit target-practiced on a live man in an open field. We had just swept through a couple of villages in the province of Tay Ninh, not too far from a field firebase from where we patrolled daily. The young soldier aimed his M-79 grenade launcher at the older man in the open field and fired it, hitting him

on the forehead and blowing his skull off. There was a brief applause, and then a couple of the soldiers walked over to get a close glimpse of the victim. As I recall the atrocious incident, I can still hear the noise the explosion made upon impact. My own dehumanized condition at the time allowed me to witness cold-blooded murder. There was no evidence to suggest the man in the field was part of any particular group considered enemy.

Other violations consisted of raping women of all ages. This was a most common activity among American GIs and was not openly condoned but practiced almost daily. There seemed to be no rhyme or reason for the behaviors; it was simply a part of our own war-psychotic virus. . . . As young soldiers, [we] had been trained and brainwashed to respond in that manner. Our ability to read the world had been constructed through the rigorous training process in basic and advanced military training. It wasn't until years later that I and thousands of others like myself began to understand the effects of the human and ecological devastation U.S. military intervention in Vietnam had caused. After I arrived home, I spent many months in therapy trying to get myself together and finally did, but it was painful and a real inner struggle. I will always have to live and struggle with the experiences I went through in Vietnam. As we know, many Vietnam veterans did not survive civilian life and ended up taking their own lives.

The Vietnam museum would also show reenactments of the mass killings of children in the so called pacification operations and put human faces on disfigured children who are still suffering the aftermath of our spraying of the defoliant Agent Orange on Vietnam. It is not only Saddam Hussein who should be put on trial before an international tribunal for his use of chemicals (against the Kurds). Agent Orange and napalm did no less harm to the people of Vietnam, and their use constitutes no less of a crime, as graphically captured by a former soldier. "They'd be out on a mission and call in strikes. Napalm would be sprayed, and the people would be burning. Sometimes they'd put them out of their misery. The guys who did that are still coming into vet centers with it 12 years later" (Gibson, 1988, p. 146).

The presence of museums for slavery, Vietnam, and American Indian genocide alongside our museums of fine arts and science museums would create a pedagogical space that not only would keep dangerous historical memories alive but also would provide a pedagogical structure that juxtaposes historical events, providing a cultural collage to force us to look at the Western cultural heritage. The juxtaposition of historical events would also enable us to develop a more critical understanding of the often mystified received historical facts, allowing us to deconstruct these facts so as to understand the reasons behind them.

These museums of crimes against humanity also would "remind us that when we embrace the Other, we not only meet ourselves, we embrace the marginal images that the modern world, optimistic and progressive as it has been, has shunned and has paid a price for forgetting" (Fuentes, 1992, p. 411).

These museums would perhaps prevent the modern world from ignoring the carnage and mass rape of women, including children as young as five years of age, in Bosnia. These museums could also serve to remind us that when we dehumanize the Other, we also dehumanize ourselves, as a Vietnam veteran succinctly points out: "When we came back after the mine sweep he [an old Vietnamese man about eighty years old] was outside his hootch. And all his relatives and friends were sitting around and crying and shit. And we laughed. And human beings don't do things like that. But we stayed there and we fucking laughed until he died. So it turns you into some sort of fucking animal" (Gibson, 1988, p. 204). The museums, like Goya's "black paintings" (Fuentes, 1992, p. 411) would serve as a constant reminder that we should always be vigilant in order to avoid complacency and the social construction of not seeing. Perhaps, Arthur Schlesinger Jr. and E. D. Hirsch, among other Western cultural legionnaires, can learn a lesson from Carlos Fuentes' insightful comments. If these critics honestly reflect on Fuentes' insights, they will come to the realization that the real issue is not Western culture versus multiculturalism. The fundamental issue is the recognition of the humanity in us and in others:

> The art of Spain and Spanish America is a constant reminder of the cruelty that we can exercise on our fellow human beings. But like all tragic art, it asks us first to take a hard look at the consequences of our actions, and to respect the passage of time so that we can transform our experience into knowledge. Acting on knowledge, we can have hope that this time we shall prevail.
>
> We will be able to embrace the Other, enlarging our human possibility. People and their cultures perish in isolation, but they are born or reborn in contact with other men and women, with men and women of another culture, another creed, another race. If we do not recognize our humanity in others, we shall not recognize it in ourselves. (Fuentes, 1988, p. 411)

References

Aronowitz, Stanley, and Henry A. Giroux. 1988. "Schooling, Culture, and Literacy in the Age of Broken Dreams: A Review of Bloom and Hirsch." *Harvard Educational Review* 58: 185.

Chomsky, Noam. 1988. *Language and Politics*. Translated by C. P. Otero. New York: Black Rose.

Fields, Robert J. 1987. *The History of the United States*. Vol. 2. New Jersey: Ammanour Corp, Book-Lab.

Fuentes, Carlos. 1992. "The Mirror of the Other." *Nation*, March 30.

Gannaway, G. 1994. *Transforming Mind*. Westport: Bergin and Garvey.

Gibson, James W. 1988. *The Perfect War*. New York: Vintage.

Hirsch, E. D., Jr., F. J. Kett, and J. Tuefil. 1988. *Dictionary of Cultural Literacy: What Every American Needs to Know*. Boston: Houghton Mifflin.

Kozol, Jonathan. 1991. *Savage Inequalities*. New York: Crown.

Miller, Alice. 1990. *For Your Own Good*. New York: Noonday.

Stannard, E. D. 1992. "Genocide in the Americas." *Nation*, October 19.

Zinn, Howard. 1990. *A People's History of the United States*. New York: Harper Perennial.

6

Labor Power, Culture, and the Cultural Commodity

Paul Willis

To discover the various uses of things is the work of history
—Karl Marx

No one really imagines any more that schools are about emancipation
for working class and subordinate groups. There is no talk of middle-
class aspirations and possibilities, only of the dull and detailed, increasingly compulsory, increasingly remedial measures felt to be necessary—alongside welfare reforms, work experience schemes, and
labor market bridging mechanisms—to try to ensure the fitness for
working, at least, of the working class. The highest ambition inculcated
into the working-class student, indeed reflecting their own desperate
needs, is for a job, often any job.

The socially reproductive function of schooling has shed its liberal
clothes and increasingly forms the main visible template for the assem-
bly of a whole jigsaw puzzle of social, juridical, welfare, economic, and
training policies. The pieces may be differently shaped, named, and ar-
ranged in different countries, but most of the puzzles share a vector of
a newly intensified attempt to regulate and prepare labor power for
insertion into capitalist labor processes on employer's terms. These
tendencies are not without marked internal contradictions, and they
will not proceed without resistances and unintended consequences of
various kinds. Not without reason, however, the promoters of renewed
control and regulation may hope to work along the grain of some of
the real fears and necessities that are part of subordinate and working-
class existence; central among these are the rigors attendant upon
those who have only their manual labor power to live by or sell, seeking a buyer under conditions of the global "oversupply" of labor, the

renewed dominance of capital, and the retreat (as well as coercive turn) of state welfare.

These are important issues deserving of the closest attention. In this chapter, though, I want to contribute to only one and slightly oblique aspect of this complex bundle of issues, to outline some important practices and processes operating in the everyday lifeworld, the lived culture, of those who are at the receiving end of "reformed" training and welfare strategies; processes that will often ironize or displace the latter's aims and intentions. For there are important changes under way in the ordinary, or common, culture of the popular classes, which will add further pressures and contradictions to how education/training develops, including an increasing marginality of schooling. Though continuing as an important site for the playing out of crucial issues, schooling may be becoming increasingly marginal to the actual formation of subjectivity, identity, and culture.

This chapter is a theoretical extension and development of some of the arguments of *Common Culture* (Willis et al., 1996), which reports the results of a Gulbenkian Foundation–supported qualitative inquiry into the informal cultural practices of young people in relation to the creative consumption and use of popular cultural items, drawing instances from style and fashion, rock and pop music, and the cultural media. In particular, I explore how some of the practices of informal culture, especially in relation to the uses made of cultural and electronic commodities, are predicated upon and help to develop the expressive and creative powers of the self, in contrast to the forms of instrumentalism and discipline on offer in the formal sector. I draw a contrast between the *expressive* labor power of the former and the *instrumental* labor power of the latter.

My basic starting point is that the self-making of culture in the popular classes takes place under changing conditions, including now the seemingly unstoppable rise of the commodization of cultural materials and of their associated electronic mediation. The old locating cultural frames—work, community, labor movement institutions—are being displaced by, or developed in complex and less centered ways in relation to, new frames of meaning: leisure, consumption, and the cultural commodity. Where before the market and market relations could be seen as external—things to be opposed, alternatives found for, or means to be found through which to survive despite—the *cultural* market increasingly becomes *the* terrain for the creative negotiation of the conditions of life. The *cultural* market is more inward with, not opposed to, culture as a way of life. Experience is not against but increasingly through *cultural* commodity relations, even when these latter express opposition, difference, or indifference to *general* commodity relations.

These changing conditions of culture and communication are not just changes in context for unchanged people to perhaps take note of or exclude; they are changed conditions for the very self-production of our humanity, for changing the essence of what we are. Just as one of the great modernist questions concerns whether schooling is a force for the emancipation or reproduction of the working class, so one of the great late-modern questions concerns whether the new cultural media, electronic and commercial, are the means of a renewed and more subtle domination, or, whether, *through the creativities of productive reception*, they might constitute new networks for semiotic possibility for subordinate groups. We'll begin to find answers, or to find complex moving equilibriums of truths, in both formulations only by looking at the real profane world as it develops now through its "bad" sides, not by stopping in self-confirming, safe, institutional circuits of traditional cultural values or assuming that the global cultural market offers only cretinization to the young working class. In particular, we need to examine very closely and in an open and experimental manner the actual social articulations and in-practice meanings of one of the prime movers of late modernization—the cultural commodity. That is the purpose of this essay.

I hope readers will bear with me through the lengthy and perhaps idiosyncratic theoretical digressions that follow in the next two sections. To try to get at the specificity and social dialectic of the commodity dynamic as it comes to dominate the cultural realm, I return to a consideration of Marx's original formulations on commodity fetishism and try to build from there toward an understanding of the cultural commodity. Later sections deal with how the informal practices of everyday culture or common culture, what I call practices of *symbolic work*, creatively take up fetishized commodity meanings and materials for their own meaning-making (see Willis, forthcoming).

The Special Nature of the Cultural Commodity

First, a little necessary exposition on the basic commodity form before we get to a consideration of its *cultural* variety. The category of the commodity is right at the heart of the Marxist system of exploring the inner workings of the capitalist system. It is where Marx starts in volume 1 of *Capital*, and an analysis of the circulation of commodities opens volume 2.

The commodity produced by the capitalist labor process appears on the market naked, as a simple object for sale. Its smooth surfaces show no sign of the social relation of exploitation that produced it or of the labor time embodied within it, which gives it exchange value on the market. It might have fallen from heaven. Forgetting its common history of production, breaking off all meaning arising from that, each object seems to be wholly independent and different from other objects, carrying meaning only in relation to possible future uses for which it may be variably suited—its use value. Commodities are alienated from each other, alienated from prior meaning, alienated from the human processes and relationships that produced them. They seem to exist only in and for themselves, they are *fetishized.*

But, of course, commodities are in fact produced in a highly specific and determinate set of histories, relations, and skills. They have not fallen from heaven. Follow any commodity back to the factory, and there is a world of surprise in store: complex labor processes, human hierarchies, discipline, sometimes bizarre management regimes of control and motivation, conflict, weariness, and often suffering too. These things we know very familiarly in what we ourselves produce or provide, but we forget them in what all others produce. This forgetting produces a fascination in commodities and in their own glistening forgetfulness and mysterious self-absorption.

Commodities are not without meaning, certainly not without future usefulness, but their meaning is strangely truncated, condensed, cut off. We struggle with our own cargo cultist mentality. Where have these perfectly formed objects come from? There's a mystery in the way in which commodities both contain (because produced by) and deny (they're only objects) wider social relations. This phenomenon of commodity fetishism is the starting point and lynchpin of Marx's analysis:

> A commodity is . . . a mysterious thing, simply because in it the social character of men's labour appears to them as an objective character stamped upon the product of the labour . . . a definite social relation between men . . . assumes, in their eyes, the fantastic form of a relation between things. Fetishism . . . attaches itself to the products of labour . . . value (i.e., capitalist production) [and] converts every product into a social hieroglyphic. (Marx, 1957, p. 42)

The use of the term *hieroglyphic* here is fascinating and illuminating. A hieroglyph is a picture sign, as in the picture script of the ancient Egyptian priesthood, a system now taken to be difficult or impossible to decode. Note the point that the commodity is already a sign, as well as a material thing, but a sign that seems to mystify and obfuscate rather than to communicate.

An analysis of the mode of production of this hieroglyph takes up the rest of volume 1 of *Capital*. Marxists have, in general, concentrated on questions of the social relations and resistances involved in capitalist production and on questions of how human labor power is itself bought and sold like a commodity. But as volume 2 of *Capital* makes clear, the commodity form is also central to the process whereby capital accumulation is realized through circulation and exchange. There, the circuit of capital is represented as M-C-P-C'-M'. Money capital (M) buys commodities (C, labor and materials) and the technical means of production (P) to manufacture new commodities of greater worth and value (C'), which are then sold to reproduce the money form, now expanded (M').

It is a supremely important precondition for the whole cycle and therefore for surplus extraction and accumulation that newly produced commodities are actually sold. The forms of the circuit must be continuously *transformed*, metamorphosis that is at the very heart of the capitalist process. There is a devilish risk that capitalists may not sell their products, that they may be left with a full warehouse. They risk this tragedy every time they produce a new batch of commodities. They must take the risk repeatedly in order to accumulate at all. The characteristic of the commodity that promises, not guarantees, this ability to fly off the shelves is its real or apparent sensuous *usefulness*, what it promises to do or satisfy in human need or desire. The exchange value of a commodity is therefore dependent on its use value. In the endless cycle of capital, the capitalist ceaselessly reinforces this characteristic—usefulness as the promise to sell—and unceremoniously turfs out what seems not to offer concrete use. This all adds to the mysterious and restless fascination of commodities; they're honed, however imperfectly, always in the direction of desire, honed always to the future of individual consumption rather than to the past of collective production. Within this general framework there are some general points I'd like to make about the nature of *cultural* commodities.

The first point is that the circuit of the transformation of capital really does concern a metamorphosis. This is the change of the money form into the cultural commodity form. These things are ontologically separate. A cultural commodity is not money in clothes. It is a cultural form. It must have existence and identity on the cultural plane if the circuit of capital is to continue to flow. Money does not make itself. The nervous capitalist is forced to unleash a metamorphosis in order to accumulate at all, but there is no way to avoid the terrible risk of the process stopping midstream, that no further transformations follow and that the cultural commodity not be turned back into (more) money. It might stop forever in its own form. The cultural commodity might not sell. Capitalists would surely sell their souls to find some magic alchemy to secretly code this form to find its way back into money every time.[1] Sadly, this cannot be. Indeed, the risks are more severe in the cultural realm. Only about one in ten films and records make any real money, but all ten have to be made in order to have the chance of making money on the one. This continuous metamorphosis of money into something quite unlike itself, which it cannot control, should rule out all simple reductions behind the texts and artifacts of capitalist cultural production to economic motives and organizations of production.

Cultural commodities are not subject to the same laws as money. They do not do the same bidding as money. They do not move the factors of production or organize social relations as does money. And if money cannot even ensure turning the commodity back into money, why should we grant it powers not even claimed, powers to so program internal textual meanings as to hold the same direct sway over receivers that money wields over workers, to make them fatal realists and to accept alienated tasks and meanings—the walking dead workers of capitalist consumption? If capitalists could really control the internal workings of the cultural commodity, the first order they would give would be for the commodity to turn itself back into money. Since this requirement is so often unfulfilled, we should have our doubts about other *social* orders. Cultural commodities make—all on their own, by their very existence—a practical distinction and separation between the social relations of production and the social relations of consumption.

A further point follows about the nature of the necessary, inevitable, and driven role of commodities in the circuit of capital. The circle is unbroken and never ending; so instead of starting the circuit with money, why not start it with commodities? Just as capital is transformed in the three stages of its life, so is the commodity transformed in three stages: market commodities are sold to produce money, which purchases commodities for productive consumption in labor processes, which produce *more* new commodities for the market (which are sold for money, etc.). Just as capital risks transformation and loss as a necessity in its own expansion, to the same degree are commodities driven to change form.

It's possible, then, to cycle forward the famous circuit of capital to produce: C-M-C-P-C'.[2] This starts and ends with commodities (C), as the usual cycle starts and ends with money (M). Just as the money at the end of the conventional cycle is a greater volume (M'), so is the commodity at the end of the commodity cycle "greater" (C'). The valorized money form of circulation is also a valorized form of *expanded* commodity circulation. Here we see a good exemplification of the very important general point, embedded in all of the arguments here, that the cultural commodity is not just a category of political economy but is equally of cultural and community meaning. As capital accumulates, so do commodities, so that they become available on an everyday basis to all (with money) in modern societies. In this regard, they are truly like the commodities of the international commodity exchanges for cereals and metals. That which was unavailable or restricted becomes an ordinary feature of the environment. In this, of course, cultural commodities are massively assisted by electronic mediation, with its multitude of one-way telephone calls "silencing the masses." Whatever the truth of this last phrase, commodification and electronification certainly bring mass *availability*.

A third supremely important point concerns the transfer of the quality of usefulness within the general form to the cultural form of the commodity. The circuit of capital concerns unlike things, although it is held together by the value form. The circuit could break down at any point, especially at the crucial stage at which commodities are sold on the market. It is the use value of the commodity that is the best guarantee of purchase, and this will be developed and emphasized at every point through the never-ending cycles. The direction of change and the nature of "accumulation" in the cultural commodity circuit must be, therefore, of the ever-refocused invitation to use. All other norms and social conventions of consumption are subordinated to the primacy of use, any possible use—whether in the brothel or in the cathedral of cultural meaning.[3] The cultural commodity is a force for the distillation of usefulness freeing up the space from inherited social dependencies.

The Struggle between the Commodity and the Code

All of the foregoing applies, actually, to the commodity qua commodity applied to its cultural case. How are we to understand the specificity of cultural commodities? What is the meaning of the *social* in their *social hieroglyph*?

I argue that what separates cultural commodities from commodities in general is the *particular* nature and quality of their usefulness. This quality is one of actual or potential *communicative meaningfulness*, the ability to enable communication of meaning from object to human and, ultimately, from human to human. The signs, symbols, and materials used in communicative commodities can operate as use values only to the extent that they are meaningful to consumers. But this is to say something very strange indeed about a commodity form. The general form that primarily breaks communication through its very fetishism—concealing its social relations of production, how and why it was made, for whom and by whom—must in this case and as its first purpose enable meaningfulness.

It is evidently necessary to separate two levels in the commodity form: its basic commodity-ness, or the bearer form, and its communicative usefulness, or its cultural code. Marx says that the commodity is, in general, a social hieroglyph. We may say, then, that the cultural commodity is a hieroglyph on a hieroglyph, an enigma within an enigma. One hieroglyph points back darkly to a hidden production, one points forward brightly to possible use. The consequences of this double, compressed, and contradictory symbolic articulation have not been adequately analyzed, both for the *complexity* it must bring to an understanding of the cultural commodity and for the possibility of impacted *contrary* decodings of the dual hieroglyphs.

Let us consider, first, what I call *simple* usefulness. The whole point about the second hieroglyph, the cultural code, is that it must be inherently more decodable (useful) than the first hieroglyph, the bearer commodity form. A potential customer might be expected to be able to imagine future use values of a "noncultural" commodity—eating food, sitting on a chair. Such use values are direct and can be understood most independently from the social hieroglyphic aspect of the general commodity form. Matters are very different in the case of finding use values for a really and intrinsically hieroglyphic hieroglyph. Mere alienated squiggles, dots, or sounds might find no customers! In order to be as certain as possible of finding customers, it is necessary to operate in some kind of cultural code, which by definition cannot be private, arcane, or special. It must be *shared* with as many customers as possible and include *communality*, some experience of *social connection*, between them and the original message producers, both of whom are participants in a community of meaning. This directly contradicts the cutting of social connection inherent within the basic commodity form, an astonishing thing in view of commodity fetishism.

The contradiction I am trying to expand upon is that, although cultural commodities are subject to commodity fetishism simply because they are commodities, they are simultaneously subject to the absolute need to defetishize themselves, simply because they are also meaning-communicative objects.

Think of the example of music. For itself, for its hieroglyphic hieroglyph nature, music is simply just noise. It is only within a shared community of communication and understanding that specific types of noise can be defined as music and that a giving up and opening of aspects of the spiritual self can be undertaken and experienced as appreciation of that music. Think of the example of sports. There's been much commentary on the commodification of football in the United Kingdom and its recently much-expanded electronic presentation, but no amount of fetishism will destroy the necessity for an assumption of football knowledge—rules, clubs, characters, folklore, fandom—in the code of the commodified text. Televised football games cannot exist apart from the football community. You could say that commodification of British football and the flotation of clubs as joint stock companies is a cynical exercise in the buying and selling of blocs of fans (their communities). But equally—my point—this commodization also recognizes community, however exploitatively, in a way that general fetishism would lead you to think was impossible.

The ubiquity and expanded nature of cultural commodity production seems to offer endless new possibilities for extending communication and community and for making their materials as legible, open, and usable as possible. Distilled usefulness drives cultural communities not only to seek and connect with communities of meaning but also to shape and enlarge them in the direction of the greater usefulness (meaningfulness to others) of their meanings. Classic FM radio has doubled the radio audience for classical music in the United Kingdom at a time when subsidized concert halls are emptying. Pavarotti's World Cup anthem brought a whole new audience to opera. The serialization of literary classics on television produces tenfold increases in book sales. The commodization of Manchester United through television exposure, sales of scarves, kits, clothes, and memorabilia has produced a community of fans (fan base for the stock market and basis of comparative capitalization) of two and a half million, far more than could ever watch a match in a real community gathering. Manchester United plans to start its own satellite TV channel, not least to tap into the huge emergent Asian market for football, so helping to produce an electronic community of many millions more.

Perhaps Hollywood's commodization of film is the paradigm case for the turning of cultural artifacts into cultural commodities through the distillation of communicative usefulness for the largest possible number. Realism is the visual lingua franca for reaching back and forth across the commodity form to find meaning and continuity. The rest of Hollywood filmic grammar pivots on convergent attempts to maximize recognizability and use: human interest, pace, identification, audience targeting, and structuring of taste and legibility through strong genre demarcation.

The general commodity form then may militate against social meaning, but it needs shared meaning when it wears its cultural clothes. One may say that capitalist culture is trying not to be capitalist. Moreover, it is the capitalist obsession of the ever-driven circuit of accumulation (remember, a commodity circuit, too), which ensures the never-ending and restless search for precisely that social connection that the capitalist commodity form denies. The uncertainty of whether the commodity will sell has to be negotiated time after time as a condition of the circuit that produces it, and it will sell only if it offers meaningful use in some shared symbolic world. The prior semiotic, material, and human factory of production of cultural commodities cannot be cut off from in the same way as the factory is from the material commodity. It is these connections that allow it to be sold at all; in the ever-repeated cycle of capital accumulation, the commodity is ever repeatedly revalorized not only with value (embodied human labor time) but also with meaning—new, extra, or more relevant meaning, meaning at any rate whose prerequisite is that sharedness that the fetishized commodity form denies.

I may seem here to be arguing that usefulness in the case of the cultural commodity, and only in the case of the cultural variant, overpowers fetishism. It is certainly important to stress the useful meaningfulness of the cultural commodity at a certain stage of the argument, to underline just what a strange and contradictory thing is this latter thing. But if the cultural commodity were indeed *all* usefulness, it would in fact cease to be a commodity. The usefulness of cultural commodities cannot actually imply a sharing of real, authentic, organic community as, for instance, that which lies behind our sense of William's whole way of life. Millions of the new Manchester United fans have never visited, and will never visit, Old Trafford. Nor does the special kind of communicative usefulness of the cultural commodity imply knowledge in the consumer of the actual industrial labor process and capital relation that reproduces the cultural commodity.

Here we come to the nub of the argument, the final, clinching specificity of the cultural commodity, which is that, actually, its usefulness must not only permanently coexist with fetishism but also be profoundly and contradictorily transformed, altered, and stressed by it. In no other commodity form are usefulness and fetishism so unifyingly opposed. Defetishization works against fetishism, and fetishism works against defetishism, producing a continuingly stable instability in the cultural commodity. This is the elusive quality I've been pursuing, the *particular* nature of the cultural commodity. We may say the *Quasimodo* commodity. Its two halves are always half formed, struggling to complete themselves but failing through the ceaseless tension arising from their other half, from which they can never escape. Hardly has a community of meaning held sway than it is extinguished by fetishism; but only by its instant renewal will the commodity perform its appointed role. Unreal advertisements surround the shows and films that seem so real; glossy book covers, which have nothing to do with what's inside, tell you that someone wants to sell to you more than to communicate with you; the way you buy an album of love songs from multiple copies in the store tells you that it was not really made for "only you." The patronizing familiarity and bogus friendliness of the disc or video jockey tells you that he is no friend, really. Conversations are cut off rudely by phone-in hosts, showing the caller that the electronic commodity community is like no real, warm community. Your purchasing power being bought and sold on the London stock market makes hardly a home of a grounds that you have never visited in Manchester.

There is then a fundamental contradiction and instability in the *doubly half-formed, Quasimodo,* cultural commodity form. It must seem to offer the shared and communal, although its very form breaks organicism, local connection, and local meaning. A hieroglyph must simultaneously be not a hieroglyph. Fetishism must defetishize itself. Lack of social connection must present itself as social connection. This is the unstable, though intrinsic, double naturing of the cultural commodity, the source of its seductive charm. Neither nature can predominate, but each will struggle against the other to the end of time. In this eternal tension, an offer of meaning is immediately cut off. The impossibility of decipherment works through ease of decipherment. Semiotic social promiscuity works through an offer of individual faith and warmth. Alienation must overcome estrangement. Here lie clues to the secret powers of cultural commodities, to their hypnotic polysemy, to the inner creative impulses they supply to those who accept their offer: Use me but do not possess me.

Here too, at last, we see why the age of the ascendency of the cultural commodity is also the age of the domination of communication by electronic means. The insistent but impossible community offered by the cultural commodity is the false immediacy of the electronic message, best exemplified in the sensuous offer of community in the realist TV image. Reach out to touch its warmth and you find only cold glass. The false, ever hopelessly self-repairing, cultural commodity makes its fraudulent offers ad electronic infinitum in every home. Forgive the determinism; but once set upon the colonization of the cultural realm, the commodity age was somehow fated to develop the electronic image, its own abstract nature made concrete.

The workings through of these contradictions of the *Quasimodo* cultural commodity in practice are complex and multiform. The blind hand of the market and the ceaseless circuitry of commodities, finding any uses that will sell them, speeds up and explores all the permutations and limits of the contradictions in concrete cases. Yet the central, locating contradiction remains common to the tensions of all possibilities. These possibilities do not simply cancel each other out, fetishism wholly negating defetishism. They produce a number of potentially positive and productive potentials of *complex usefulness*, the usefulness of fetishized usefulness.[4] Fetishism may truncate meaning, but it simultaneously makes what remains more open, contestable, and "sticky." I discuss these complex usefulness possibilities under the headings of loss of dependency, displacement, and subversion.

Loss of Dependency

In the dominant register, commodity communication is impure and inferior, lacking in seriousness and moral purpose. It lacks the Reithian imperative to educate as well as to inform and entertain. There is, however, a subtext of advantage unseen to dominant eyes, which allows, in some respects, the freer passage of new information. The *Quasimodo* naturing of the cultural commodity allows social information and a social semiotic to get through to receivers/viewers/users without social dependency—except, of course, and very importantly, that of the immediate cash nexus and of the sacrifices necessary to get to it. Fetishism's restraint and half-forming power over its unfetishized other half *strips off*, to some degree, the guilty baggage of historical connotation from communicative meaning; strips it of limiting and dependence-inducing prior social relationships, including the specification of given, historically accreted, norms of consumption and use.

The authority of other communication types actually assumes a deference or semiotic powerlessness in receivers, who are assumed to be subordinate in the social relationship that holds the communication. Institutional–educational communication carries an obvious paternalism, even an implied compulsion. Auratic communications (as in works of art emitting an aura) are explicitly authoritarian in locating all meaning in the text and in severely prescribing relevant norms for consumption and decoding. Even community meanings carry a responsibility toward those who have communicated—or what is spoken of in the immediacy and reciprocity of what is bounded by the sharedness of meaning. By contrast to all these, the meanings of cultural commodities come without guilt, apparently without historical let or hindrance, positively reeking of the democracy of the brothel, inviting their prostitution by potent, independent users.

Cultural commodities must deal in social meaning and connection, but they do not enforce *particular* meaning. They are without organized semiotic policing (apart from the imperatives of the commodity form itself, of course). They make human offers but no contracts. They travel without passports. Though carrying over the semiotic and symbolic resources from the circumstances of their formation, cultural commodities are without the limits, dependencies, guilts, and carry-overs of moral control attendant on these circumstances. The messages and meanings that survive to new contexts are social without being socially overdetermined, without being fixed, by the social field forces of their original location. New contexts really can make old texts new.

So only commodity communication offers community meanings without community. Only it offers the hand of meaning without a stick of authority in the other. Only it offers amnesia for the sacred and passage for the profane. Commodity meanings that survive beyond fetishism are maximally open to finding new articulations, new homes. Distance and place are abolished in these solicitations. Meanings can carry from the far corners of the Earth as easily as they can from around the corner: Manchester United fans in Manchuria, black rhythm and blues in Liverpool, London's East Enders in Manhattan, Brazilian soaps with Italian pasta. Here is a material base for understanding the compressions of time and space, the disorientations, the disjunctions between place and home, the apparently free floatingness of discourses: things labeled *postmodern* as if that was explanation enough for them being conjured out of thin air.

Displacement

Fetishism corrupts the possibility of simple usefulness within particular or named, real, sensuous communities of meanings. It interrupts the code, but the desperate bid to find any social connection across the bridge of fetishism leads to a promiscuous displacement of meaning onto as many other bearer forms as possible. The half message left in the communicative bit of the commodity, split off from its real community home by fetishism, seeks imaginary community in any other kind of human activity, value, solidarity, or worth. Electronic football becomes entertainment or a new aesthetics for the middle class or the giant screen community of a pub or club.

In news and current affairs, meaning is diffused across as many other uses and categories, across as many implied or imagined communities, as possible, to make as many contacts with receivers as possible beyond the purpose of simply to inform. So the newscaster becomes a friend and guide, the program a neighborhood get-together with human interest and "to end with" or "and finally" items emphasizing imaginary solidarity, with ambulance and police car chasing emphasizing human sensation, shock, and horror, in case the viewer's senses have drifted momentarily during a previous, more purely information, item that could not be imbued with some other value or meaning. Public broadcasting is not exempt. A recent secret report drawn up by senior BBC executives, called "Reflecting the World," suggests including entertainment stars into news reporting because "the groups at the bottom are looking for entertainment, not information." BBC weather forecast stalwarts are being dropped as broadcasters switch to a "more entertaining" American format.

The search for home or community leads not only to the hijacking of other existing communities of meaning, expressive practices, or human values but also to the opening up of new ones by adding or greatly expanding (perhaps there are no wholly noncommunicative human uses), the communicative or expressive dimension of the use values of other commodities. A culturalizing process seeks and finds whole new branches of productive application by suggesting new, other, or more developed social meanings for functional objects, to give other reasons than their immediate usefulness for buying them, driving an abstract content into other forms to increase their prospects for cultural useful-ness—*imbuing* them with communicative usefulness.

Communicative or expressive usefulness seeks to be embedded in other kinds of usefulness: noncoded, residually coded, or sensuous. This produces a kind of coding in the embued item, though always ma-terial and mixed and not of the floating signifier type. From the com-municative side—whatever is doing the embuing—there is a decoding or dedigitalizing or dearbitrizing of a code; the possessing, literally, of other entities: bodies, practices, things, uses, materials. In such ways, cultural commodities find and make whole new and changing markets out of a previous cycle of commodization. Manchester United has found a whole new market for clothing and memorabilia. Purchasing a car is also to purchase a life statement. Perhaps the whole of the mod-ern advertising industry is about seeking to further *imbue,* or cultural-ize, objects that may have only limited functional physical uses, to asso-ciate them with other meanings, to make them to some degree expressive. Under modern conditions perhaps, there are no noncultur-alized objects; that is, objects that signify only their own direct uses and satisfactions. The culturalization of commodities is now a condi-tion of our culture and is the way we make sense of ourselves and others.

The desperation to find a sensuous base for fetishized communica-tion in the proffer of imaginary community meaning, and to see in all sensuous activities and uses the possibility of embuing them with com-munity and meaning, produces a tendency to focus on the expressive and cultural properties of the human body. The body and how it is seen is, so to speak, the smallest unit of communicative practice, the immovable material resting place, for the possibility of lodgement of fraudulent community. Here is one of the main mechanisms of detraditionalization, one of the main mechanisms of the rise of individuation as the hallmark of late or post modernism, especially as the *somatization* of individual meaning in an emergent, more body-based, structure of feeling in commodity culture.

Unconsciously and blindly, not willed or knowing, commodification of communication seeks to embody usefulness in as many body-oriented and immediate ways as possible. Commodities insinuate themselves into the interstices of daily life and in and around the somatic natures and tactile presence of the human body. Commodity-related meanings are therefore likely to be tied up with libidinous meanings in complex ways, both as a materialism of desire (what actually turns you on) and as a projection of the self as materially desirable to others. The marketing and design of the fetishized use values of fashion glamor and hygiene products invite us to sell ourselves like commodities to each other—in actual use, tempered toward enhancing the sensuousness (usefulness) of actual warm bodies in real relationships, in which, however, remaining fetishisms add distance and exploitation to personal relations, a mystery and objectification never to be fully overcome but which may aid desire.

The imbuement of the body and concrete practices with meaning looking for completion also aids in the globalization of the commodity culture; embued semicodes travel where purely arbitrary digital–alphabetical ones cannot.

Subversion

The double enigma of the *Quasimodo* cultural commodity form produces not only a struggle of one part against another—commodity as usefulness, commodity as fetishism—but also, as we have seen, of this communicative part (usefulness) within itself. The effect of the bearer form (the fetishism of the general commodity form) on the communicative code is to partially fetishize and distance the latter's internal forms. Of course, the communicative code cannot be completely fetishized; otherwise, it would not communicate. But the instability between the forms gives a good nudge *within and without* the text to understand the fetishistic nature of the form, thus subjecting its surviving internal meaning to irony, relativism, and even subversion. Football fandom can never be the same after the flotation of Manchester United. The usefulness bit of the argument and balance of contradiction, though, should not be forgotten, nor should the way this produces its handmaiden of realism, nor should the fact that usefulness is never dissociated from fetishistic loosening of immediate identities, not least in realistic representation. Viewers and listeners may be presented with the familiar and knowable, but the commodity form ensures, both internally and externally, that it can never be taken as authentic and original.

The productivity in reception of simple usefulness in texts may be along a grain of realism and realist decodings. But the *complex usefulness* of cultural commodities also offers the productivity of immediate subversion. In the days of representative innocence, the experts could have fund dissecting how the rest of us were manipulated semiotically. But now these simple investment returns to an elite have been crowded out by the speculations of the mass. We are all practical experts on mythologies now, on how to read the codes in cultural literacy, on how to take the broad hint when the advertisements' inside and outside texts tell us that nothing is real. When there's no one left who believes what they're told, there's no point in deconstruction. Realism subverts realism in the commodity relation.

The Commodity: The Symbolic Work of Information Culture

People make their own culture, but to paraphrase Marx, they do it under conditions and *with materials* not of their own making. It is the materials, and their uses, that I am focusing on in this chapter. These are now overwhelmingly, especially for the popular classes, commoditized materials.

Common Culture (Willis et al., 1996) gives many examples of the creative practices around young peoples' uses of cultural commodities and the electronic media. Young people are able to select, combine, and recombine chosen elements from an enormous range of received symbolic material and appropriate them to their own concerns and feelings. Often, they assemble new symbolic wholes. This is particularly evident in the active mining by the young of forty years or so of popular music history; in the production of off-air tapes, circulated to an extent that has precipitated a crisis of copyright in the recording industry; and in the creativity of fashion and popular style. In such ways, young people demonstrate the ability to appropriate and recontextualize provided materials to express personal and often profound feelings and meanings of their own.

Consumption is still often seen as passive and manipulated, a mechanistic reflection of the cynicism and debasement of the manner and motive of production of what is consumed. In *Common Culture,* I use the term *symbolic work* to focus on the *active* and *productive* nature of practices of consumption, wherein meanings are assembled or derived from a variety of symbolic materials, now centrally including the fragments and flows of a commoditized, electronic environment, in order to make whole, or to bring greater coherence to, sets of personal and collective meanings in particular structured context. Symbolic work is comparable to but less alienated than wage labor. It involves Marx's famous element of the humble architect raising structures in imagination and is a form of work as self-realization. Historically, commodity production may have driven out from the inside of the labor process the pride in skill and craft that it now welcomes back and needs in the outside world of (productive) cultural consumption.

Symbolic work concerns symbolic understanding and manipulation, meaning-making and sense-making, a centripetal force to place against the now mandatory decenteredness of the subject. As in the material capitalist labor process, production takes the form of the transformation of commodities—their productive consumption through the expenditure of human labor power to produce expanded value. This expanded value arises from the productive exploitation of the prior use value of commodities and takes the form of an expansion of that use value, that is, making the cultural object more useful, especially in connecting and converting general, alienated, and fetishized meanings into local, specific, contextual meanings and satisfactions of a kind not available locally before. This can be seen as an increase of use value over exchange value in the commodity, of conversion of estrangement into belonging, of the decommodization of the commodity.

My specific point is that all of these processes presuppose and help to produce a broad, humanist, and expressive subjective sense and practice of the labor power that is doing the work, in stark contrast to the narrow, instrumental models inscribed within training or state forms of the regulation and attempted formation of labor power. Though working with alienated materials, this *expressive* labor power is less alienated at least within its own bounds than is *instrumental* labor power; it works at home (cf. Marx, "He [the worker] is at home when he isn't working, and when he is working he is not at home") in ways that enable its owner's own dreams and plans to be at least partly recognized, not least in the affirmation and development of the very *possibility* of the exercise and future expansion of expressive powers.

In some very important ways, cultural commodities are highly suited to adoption within the symbolic work of informal cultural production. The promiscuous and ubiquitous fetishized object (unlike the scarce auratic object) offers as many clues as possible for its own (ultimately impossible within its own circuit) dehieroglyphization. Cultural commodities are self-programmed with permanently open address systems. False offers and illusions pile on fraudulent intimacies. Intrinsic imperatives to profane use (the opposing force to aura) suppress all possible limiting norms of consumption. The ever-renewed existence of the fetishized object as a communicative commodity predicates any or all possible use of imagination or desire long enough at least to shift it off the shelf. A general satisfaction of desire is somehow on offer, a particularly elusive element of the attractive mystery of commodities, but so is specific use and apparent concrete contact. All fraudulent points on the compass of human desire are charted—and at the same time, if possible. This cacophony of possibility may upset the purist and pollute authenticity. Think of the visual clutter of Main Street, USA. Multiple temptation, evident sensation, and sheer tackiness insult the "improving heart" still beating within even the most left-wing breast. But however brutal may be these insults to refined sensibilities, they also do everything possible to suggest, pump, prime, encourage, even bully into *use*.

More unexpectedly, the fraudulence (inescapable fetishism) of the commodity form also has its uses for informal production. It accomplishes the suspension of guilt and moral context as determined by others. Destroying the reverence with which symbolic forms are viewed for a practice of profane use is the backhanded cultural contribution of commodity production. Tawdry it may be, but here are grounds for understanding one late-modern route into everyday practices of creativity and meaning-making. Contradictorily, the "homeliness-less-ness" of cultural commodities can liberate use values in concrete and contextual practices. Textual contradictionness can loosen up meanings, preparing them for reattachment in the real local meanings of actual receivers, listeners, viewers, and so on.

So even though, perhaps because, commoditized meanings are fetishized, they are actually highly suited to informal meaning-taking and meaning-making within lived everyday culture. Fetishism produces an estrangement, a lack of home, a loss of parentage and loyalty, which solicits any use, any possible attachment in a guiltless, never-ending offer of semiotic promiscuity. They indecently invite in a communicative antifetishism. Fetishism cuts the past; antifetishism opens the future. Cultural commodities have a "stickiness" for lived meanings *because* of their depthlessness.

You could say that commoditized meanings are predigested, premanualized, preexperientialized in highly appropriate ways for use in living cultures, which derive their own embedded meanings from the specific relation of sensuous parts rather than from concentrated linguistic expression. Cultural commodification seeks communicative usefulness without precondition and so finds a meeting point in practices and uses of the widest kind, not understanding themselves as being about, but nevertheless dealing in, meaning. There is an unholy, or you might say holy, fit between commodities struggling with their own fetishism and varieties of exploratory cultural and living arts practices seeking embedded communication. Lived cultural forms accept the invitation (overlooked or refused by others) to promote the internal tendency of defetishization of the cultural commodity into an external reality of real social defetishization, of social art. Lived cultural forms complete some strange new communities of meaning underneath the noses of an uncomprehending, though presiding, capitalist system.

My case then, with respect to the general cultural commodity form, is that it contains an inescapable tension, a sprung bow of exclusion and possibility. The internal signs of the cultural commodity are not simply polysemic in some inert or mechanical or matrix way. They are internally dynamic, internally contestable, internally tensed in ways that incite a response: to repair their wounded meanings. They are a distinct category of things in the world, not codes, but not not-codes. They are sensuous expressive forms that invite bodily and somatic forms of knowing and use. Just as the sacred auratic object glowers at mismatch, the commodity leers at it. It has half severed itself from its own too-insistent meanings. The mismatching of informal production finds and binds severed ends and in different ways in different circumstances. Think of how symbolic resources from the very different context and history of black American culture have been offered through commercial music to British white working-class culture, informally cut, edited, and taken up there for different purposes, without condition, without guilt, without historical baggage. The alienated offer of meaning in the commodity object is quite different from the command of cathedral understanding in the auratic object and can be taken into many homes.

Of course, the immediate qualifications are necessary again. None of this is to argue that all is for the best in the symbolic best of all possible cultural worlds. We are still no nearer to true depth in usable information for all, no nearer to the genuine understanding of other cultures in context. There are practices and materials toward a 3-D view of daily life and its dilemmas but not toward a 3-D view of the real political economy or the conditions that make up the everyday arena. The strange and alienated democracy of signs that feed the informal production of meaning was born contradictorily out of an undemocratic communications market (concentration of power, rising accumulation, etc.). Certainly, the rise of semiotic democracy is no more about economic democracy than was the rise of political democracy; there, a thousand signs fired at us everyday from advertisers. But try firing back just one, put up one humble fly poster, and you'll find yourself fired and reporting to the local police station every week for a year. Still, the reality of the daily circulation of usable symbols within the flows of trash and the daily scope for creative meaning-making as ordinary events should not be made invisible simply because they do not fit the templates of our idealist precommodity dreams.

Even if there are difficulties in its recognition and conceptualization, the reality of informal symbolic work, the values it produces, are evident in two striking ways. First, embodied labor time increases potential use values of cultural objects as they are embedded in real practices in concrete contexts. Some of the practices include selection; combination; recombination; cutting and mixing; presentation; personal and personally appropriated fashions, musics, styles; personals edits and collections. The realization of embedded value, here, can be through the medium of informal exchange in informal groups and protocommunities, the passing around and sensuous use and exploitation of technical equipment: matermixes; off-air tapes, copies, pirates; ideas for dress, recombinations of styles, and new appropriations. The scope and importance of these informal exchanges among the young should not be underestimated and is a main vector of their chosen interests and activities. Just as Marx insists that exchange is the sine qua non of surplus realization, so the manifest evidence of exchange and realization in the informal cultural sector demonstrates a prior process of *real* value production. The informal circuits are evidently driven by the value at stake, just as is the formal commodity circuit, but without the money moment. Personal and informal symbolic work produces multifarious forms of new value that, although unseen by the formal world, is made evident through continuous informal exchange.

Second, the existence of this value is most conclusively demonstrated, perhaps, by the way in which the capitalist cultural commodity circuit keeps dipping back into the streets and trawling the living culture for ideas for its next commodity, its next circuit. Capital's cultural producers remorselessly ransack the everyday in their never-ending search to find, embody, and maximize all possible use values in products. The usefulness of the new or more developed communicative forms produced and shared in real informal communities of meaning is precisely the quality that attracts the predators, even as they deny it by plunging into further commodity relations. Evidently, the formal circuit would not keep returning to the streets unless it found real value there. This is the capitalist attempt to realize the value of informal production in the traditional capitalist form of money. This has not been adequately factored into the political economy of the circuit of capital.

Penetrations in the Postmodern World

What are the implications of the arguments advanced here for the nature and meaning of communication in newly developing ways of life? Are there any genuinely *social* and *critical*, as distinct from private and individual, meanings at play? Has my position lapsed into its own kind of fetishized, private, subculture, characterized by solipsist and idealist forgetting?

I would argue that we need new ways of understanding the revelatory qualities of informal cultural production. This will not, now, be in the form of any one settled discursive representation (or cultural complex of representations) of important external relations in the world claiming superiority (or having interpretive claims made on its behalf) over others. Rather than looking for how new representations may reflect social meanings and social position, we may have to look for eruptions and disruptions in the very materials in which representations are shaped and for changes in the sensuous human capacities, the kind of labor power that is involved in their development and use *as expressions*. Even if we cannot yet determine criteria for the epistemological superiority of any truth claims embedded there, the practices of informal production will nevertheless continue without us, making their own priorities and choices, shifting their own fields, choosing their own sites for contestation. What are some of the possible categories that will be burst in the development of *expressive* labor power?

The claimed creativities for productive consumption in *Common Culture* may seem trivial in a larger social frame. And yet we find something different if we direct *ethnographic* attention to the practical moment of sensuous activity. For themselves, these practical forms of activity can be seen as far from conservative, as actually a bursting of categories. Foremost perhaps, and crudely, they burst the category of the passive receiver, of fetishism in consumption, of the consumer taking in uncritically whatever meanings seem to be inscribed within cultural commodities. More ambitiously, and theoretically more adventurously, it can be claimed that these practical activities accomplish this not in primitive or naive assertion but in bursting the bounds of a formal *textual* aesthetic.

The traditional or institutional aesthetic has been firmly reified and cut off from human process; it is "in" things—paintings, pictures, texts, scores. The "protective" and "supportive" institutions have produced this execution of meaning. Galleries and museums produce the aesthetic distance, both physical and symbolic, that selects and separates art from daily life. The institution not only selects and distances but also places objects at the epicenter of concern—unique, timeless objects emitting their own aura. And it is the object, this auratic object, that is the timeless guarantee of, ironically, human meaning and value. But appreciating the aura, decoding the timeless code, is a specialist's task. Not everyone has the eyes and ears—and training. A disposition toward fine things is necessary, possessing the right antenna and developing a sensibility to interpret the incoming signals, requiring, of course, a long liberal arts training in the conventions and equivalences of the code. All of this helps to produce and reproduce the distance, scarcity, and fixedness of traditional and institutional culture. Still, at its center, anchoring the whole thing, is the holy auratic object valorized by its internal aesthetic.

Contrastingly, the multiple and heterogeneous performances of common cultural consumption puts human activity at its heart. Whether we like them or not, as we have seen, the central imperative of the formation of the cultural commodity is that it shall be used. This is the sine qua non of the commodity, just as we may say that the sine qua non of the auratic object is that it shall not be used. Common culture reacts to and exploits this property of openness in the raging commodity, where official culture turns away into timelessness.

It may be the very homelessness and dirtiness of informal production (reflecting the alienation of the commodity) that guarantee its perpetual motion and inoculate against the insidious creeping auras of things absorbing back into themselves the human properties that made them. This can be seen as a bursting of a boundary, the stock in trade of textual modernism for most of the twentieth century (high art, bricolage, surrealism, deconstruction) is now part of everyday cultural practice. Although modernism as textual formalism preserved in institutions functions to reproduce social and cultural divisions and to make cultural elites socially unconnected, thus widening the gulf between mental and manual labor, popular practices function sensuously from the manualist side to break down that division. Modernism as institutional textual formalism offers a fraudulent, minority, and romantic escape at night from that bureaucratic, technological, commercial juggernaut that the same elites oil and service by day, as it empowers the commodity to rip on through the settled cultures of centuries without so much as a daylight word against it. In popular practice, it forces through the dialectic of *living* modernization in the ordinary experience of the majority.[5]

The practiced abilities of a developing, *expressive,* labor power developed through the productive consumption of cultural commodities demonstrate that labor power is, indeed, a commodity like no other and is capable of almost infinite application and extension. This is a sensuous basis for suspicion that not only is the capitalist purchase of labor power for a low fixed price an unfair exchange but the repetitive and disciplined uses to which it is put mark a limitation rather than an extension of human possibility. The inhuman use of labor power in wage labor counterpoints its expressive use in leisure, threatening to reignite old, as well as fire up new, themes of human alienation.

The expressive self is also a force to burst reification in official and institutional communication. It is a specific source of a practical critique of, or a particular dissatifaction with, the technical and instrumental communications of work and other bureaucratic sites. The creative uses of provided materials open up the prospect of detaching meaning from provided vertical channels and axes to allow a lateral circulation of signs and symbols relatively freer from domination in general. The expressive self teaches how to treat others as more fully human, as other expressive selves, and so must embody if not express a wider critique of how vertical structures seek to prevent or control personal meaning.

Finally, there is another disruption of categories intrinsic to the possibility of the functioning of expressive subjects, an outcome as well as a precondition for a postcommodity production of informal meaning. This is a bursting of the unitary social subject *from within*, a move toward what can be termed as the semiotic differentiation of the subject, the birth of semiotic individualism. This is the awareness, at some level beyond the identity innocences of the inculcations of *instrumental* labor power, that the self is continuously made and remade individually and collectively rather than being inherited or arising from the necessities of capitalist work and organization.

Though I argue that the productive consumption of commodities concerns a move toward their defetishization, a reconnection through praxis to locality and meaning, this more organic connection can never be that of precommodity cultures. Such (more) local meanings, and therefore the sensibilities associated with them, are not innocent. This is enforced by the nature of the impacted double hieroglyph, the enigma within the enigma of the cultural commodity. The commodity code, its fetishism, challenges the cultural code the moment that it offers safety and home. Irony saturates even the most down-home use of what can never finally be "at home." The commodity form itself operates to the other side of its limits (the opposite side to usefulness and friendliness) to preserve an element of strangeness, even as the cultural part of the cultural commodity finds new homes in and through the practices of informal symbolic work. So although the productive consumer is creatively called forth in order to reassemble the safety, to repair the gaping hole in the cultural commodity by defetishizing it in relation to personal meaning, the completion of the project is always prevented or delayed. This eternal dance and perpetually renewed elongation underline the role of artifice. Both the relocation to a personal meaning landscape and the failure of it to root fully like "natural" symbolic flora and fauna produce a loss in semiotic innocence as belief in the transparent reflection of reality in signs.

Popular cultural texts themselves now play on this. They are internally aware of artifice, they tell of their own construction in an almost Brechtian way. Self-conscious cleverness, punning, and cross-references are legion in modern advertising. It is no particular feat any more to be able to tell the difference between artifice and reality. And as advertising differentiates its markets, so it differentiates among the ties of the symbolic to the real—on the one hand, providing conflicting and cross-cutting appeals, or hails, to the subject; on the other hand, providing conflicting views about which products can do what for whom. In the practical recognition that all claims cannot be true, the differentiated cultural subject is born or strengthened.

Not only this, but advertising for the same classes of products changes over time ("You must try the new improved . . ."), contradicting itself, and so teaching us about variable desire rather than fixed need. New products betray old products, as we discover we do not really "need" the originals. New (false) meanings usurp previous (therefore false) meanings. Newly peddled desires negate old "authentic" desires. Subjectivities are not actually reassembled every time a new product appears, but they are differentiated with respect to representation. People do not believe everything they see and hear and so are under permanent pressure to assemble a semiotic working world and its possibilities for themselves, to make a new ordering of personal signification as ordinary events.

The repairing of the commodity, its defetishization in concrete local productive consumption, *is* the rearticulation of reality as it is lived and perceived by the sensuous human subject. Reality is moved, to however small a degree, by the expressive work of the labor of expressive self-making. That reality was not there in the same way before the personal work of the defetishization of the cultural commodity. The impacted double nature of the commodity sign and its built-in conflict over what is truly signified invites symbolic awareness. Here is a practical recognition that "all the world's a stage" and the productive consumer "a player on it." The spaces and contradictions and desperate incompleteness of the cultural commodity invite in symbolic subjects, but only if they exercise at least some autonomy, an autonomy that punctuates old naivetes. The creativities of informal production carry over the marks of alienation from the commodity and cannot forget the lessons learned during the endless struggle to dehieroglyphize the hieroglyph, to release an enigma from an enigma, to attend the strangeness of an alienated birth of nonalienation.

There is a powerful experiential basis here for personal differentiation from other symbolic structures—of the self and its powers of labor from prescribed roles, for instance (worker, mother, citizen, pupil)—that are clapped on social subjects from the outside. There is also the basis for a practical recognition of the self as a cultural producer, with interests developed through self-activity, for an awareness of others, mediated through the knowledge that they too produce themselves, and for a sensitivity to reality as, at least in part, a multiple collective production of social identities. Social relations between semiotically differentiated subjects are likely to be conscious of artifice, of play, of alternatives, of muted, implicit, or tacit knowledge that things, in micro at least, could have been different.

Repairing the meaning of commodities is a sensuous and practical democratic lesson (if not a cognitive or ideological recognition) that representations and symbols in general do not just unproblematically reflect a prior reality; they are *made* to connect. Just as there is an understanding of the scope for some "construction out" of the self during symbolic work, so there is the possibility for resistance against "construction in" of social classification of identity and labor power from the outside. This is also a practical basis for an alertness to the ways in which larger systems of social representation—of race, class, gender, sexuality, region, age—function not only to reflect a prior, given, reality but also to oppressively shape it, even to produce aspects of it. Not only resistance to these things but also an internal role in their shaping become further possibilities. If this shaping boils down to artifice, then not consciously but as a logic of a practice, this artifice can be enjoined.

Preexisting social representations are meanings systems and, therefore, find their way into, indeed are always already part of, meaning commodities. There is an exciting possibility here. Embedded as they are in cultural commodities, they are therefore equally subject to the latter's internal contradictions, double-naturing, and openness to symbolic work. The commodity form here operates to limit and disturb the meaning content of social representations, sloughing away the naturalness of their origins, preventing a naturalization in their destinations. Social representations therefore need not be resources only for dominant groups; cultural commodities, or their creative uses in context, must be understood as bearing a wider social valency as well as a semiotic one. The meanings not only of commodities but also of wider systems of social representation can to some extent be challenged, borrowed, and adapted to purpose in the workings of informal cultural production.

All consumption is cultural to some extent (and therefore to do with meaning, and therefore to do with social representation), but cultural commodities are more related to the sensuous, the tactile, the micro-emotive—to the direct sculpting, changing, and projecting of the human body and its intimate styles of being and relating. These somatic contacts of consumption as well as associated modes of symbolic work must therefore work through the particular nature of solid warm bodies and their differences. The points of contact of this sensuous immersion may overlap with, but are not the same as, the theorist's drily classified categories: race, class, gender. They are points on a personal map of positive distinction from others and materials toward possible personal constructions (body out, not society in) of the self as powerful, not placed; as sexy, sexual, and desirable, rather than controlled. Or at least materials toward shifting the balances from the latter to the former of these terms. There is a sensuous basis here for social subversions of received, allocating, and repressive regulation of *instrumental* labor power, its putative formation of a narrow sensuousness of the body. Informal symbolic work can be a somatic working outward against—or at least holding or ironically embarrassing—external domination and social positioning.

The age of commodity domination has brought all kinds of defeats, disruptions, and distortions, but it also makes unstable received systems of cultural identity and social representation, rendering highly problematic instrumental and labor-oriented versions of these things. The unstable energies of the double enigma taken up into concrete practices create unexpected channels for identifications to slither, for readaptations, for turnings back, for ironizations of official and regulated models. A cutting edge of subversion arises from the instability of the commodity in relation to the differentiated subject as expressive self. New mobilizations and self-representations of the expressive self may be "dirty," rather than politically correct. They may be packed with ironic and unintended consequence, but they make old-fashioned and visibly repressive the instrumental and nonironic disciplines and technologies of the attempted production of *instrumental* labor power.

We may also find in these considerations more productive ways to approach the stale antinomies of the question of the quality of arts and cultural activities. Not what is the best because most beautiful, perhaps, so much as what is best because most symbolically productive, most promoting of a popular and practicized capacity for *symbolic* work, what *in practice* shifts rather than reproduces narrower versions of the powers of the self.

Hegemony

We need to redraw the map of how we conceptualize, in general, the relations between the classes at a cultural level. As new, or more focused and rationalized, state cultural offensives seek to discipline and form the labor capacities and sensibilities of working-class and subordinate groups in rather narrow and backward-looking ways, there has arisen the possibility of new orderings of signification in ordinary experience that capsize conventional notions of hegemonic cultural domination.

As old stabilities decline, new stabilities form out of the contending forces. The odd thing about the emergence or enhancement of informal symbolic work and the associated development of *expressive* labor power is that, while tending toward independence from or critique of the dominant capitalist mode of production, it is also quite capable of embracing it, in ghostly, backward, and unintended ways. Some surprising inversions and reverses of polarity are possible, the seeing of the same things differently. Specifically, there can be a reversal in the orders of human re-creation, what has been seen as necessary to recreate the human power to labor. For the dominant mode of production nonwork, or leisure, is simply a time for recuperation, for regaining the power to labor again in the capitalist labor process; nighttime leisure and recreation supply the commodity, labor power, for daytime production. The informal mode of production inverts this. So called leisure is *the* field of real work and real production. It is, in fact, day work (waged labor) that (through the power of the wage on the cultural market) supplies the means and reproduces the possibility of applying sensuous and nonalienated labor power to symbolic production at night. Wage labor provides the only, or best, access to cultural commodities. The availability of cultural commodities for productive consumption is a sine qua non of the informal production process, just as the availability of fresh labor power is a sine qua non of the capitalist labor process. This fundamental shift can produce what I termed (Willis, 1983; see also Willis, 1981) a destressing of certain fundamental critical concerns and a transformation in how oppressive categories are seen so that they appear in a different and much less threatening light and context.

Waged work, along with its sacrifices, disciplines, and solidarities, can be seen as no longer the central axis of existence or meaning, with all else as its humble servants. Waged work is perhaps more the humble servant to keep another kind of production running smoothly. The recreations necessary, the factors of production required, for each type of production can be seen as complements, not hierarchies of oppression. Work for one is leisure for the other. Equipping labor power for the tasks of leisure is work for the other. The orders of signification are contrary and overlap the same external items but produce different interpretations of them. Has the looking glass world finally arrived? Perhaps, but not in the phantasms of postmodern theorists, in their purely discursive worlds (all the world's a page), but in the material lock of what can be thought of as opposing modes of production, as they are sensuously perceived and lived.

Of course, these locks are highly lopsided and varied according to circumstance and possibility. But their consequences can be profound. The divisions and oppressions arising from the traditional mode of production, and the orderings of meanings between the base, the superstructure, the commodity, and labor power (no matter how we may agonize over their definition and relation) may simply have no salience in informal production—and less than before within the traditional mode considered within its ghostly embrace. Indeed, far from paid work relations and oppressions needing to be ideologized through those central categories of the Marxist system, the "fair day's pay" and "freedom and equality" under the law to sell one's labor power to the highest bidder, they may simply be suffered gladly as the price of entry to the informal mode of production: the means of recreating the power of nonalienated labor. Not freedom of contract and equality under the law for the wage laborer but access to tools and materials for the development of *expressive* labor power. Freedom and equality for the expressive self! Perhaps Ayatollah Khomeini was right when he said that "the economy is for donkeys"! There are higher things than the grimy business of earning a living in the material labor process: not religion, but perhaps something rather similar though less mystical, more rational, and attuned to rather than escaping from modern conditions—the personal production of the expressive self. In this perspective, unemployment is an oppression not only or even mostly because of exclusion from paid work or even because of the poverty it produces, abstractly understood, but because of the exclusion it may bring from informal expressive production.

Not to be overlooked either is that the production of the expanded expressive self through the productive consumption of cultural commodities (for many, more forming and influential than schooling, especially for members of subordinate groups) is also simultaneously the production of labor power for possible application to formal capitalist labor processes. This is a volatile, *expressive,* labor power, which may be too developed, high aiming, and restless—surplus in its personal meanings—to fit in with the technical and repressive disciplines of many labor processes. On the other hand, the very mode of its production and expansion might limit or sideline any explicit dissatisfaction or practical discontent or unruly behavior at work. At the same time, whole branches of industry and new branches of industry, particularly the consciousness and cultural sectors, require new sources of supply of exactly such expanded-value labor power, even as deepened regulation and discipline, for the working class and subordinate groups at least, reduce the hope of garnering it from the formal education and training structures.

All of this is to suggest the necessity for exploring new, lopsided, and cynical balances in how hegemony might be operating currently, a balance in which paid work may not be the main or only axis and in which capitalist formations reproduce themselves, or at least remain grittingly stable, for reasons their elites do not understand and that have decreasingly little to do with the functioning and reform of progressively delegitimized dominant institutions. Rather than passing messages down, or confidently and coercively organizing them from above, ruling bloc social groups and institutions may be the uncomprehending beneficiaries of messages and semiotic organization passed unconsciously upward.

The strangest thing is that some aspects of subordinate agency seem to find some scope for the dynamic exercise of choice and social development in *symbolic* structures and cultural collectivities rather than in material structures and conventional orders of power. The contradiction is that tumbling in the trash of a fetishized consumer society are materials, usable as no others in terms of actual conditions and potentials for use, for moments and movements of freedom and counterfetishism, for the release and development of *expressive* labor power. Here different wisdoms are practicized, always provisional, always contingent, strangely orchestrated through the cultural commodity: that human powers and potentials are not exhausted by and cannot be contained in the capitalist definition of labor power; that surplus meaning is created by the capitalist system just as surely as is surplus value; that fetishism in cultural commodities can burst the aura of sacred objects; that nonalienated work is possible with alienated materials; that emerging *expressive* subjects will not be contained by official definitions and practices, no matter how coercive they become.

I would like to put on the education/training map the emergent contradiction between the state's multifaceted attempt to reform labor power in a more *instrumentalist* and subordinate role to the interests of productive capital and the development of an *expressive* labor power within the everyday pores of the informal culture's inhabitation of consumer capital relations. Here the *Quasimodo* cultural commodity that connects, over the narrow bridge of fetishism, original communities of meaning-making with new located communities and practices of meaning-making plays a crucial mediating role. Relations of production call forth instrumentalism, relations of consumption call forth expressivism. These two tendencies in the formation of labor power, one formal, one informal, may be parallel or in conflict or in different local complex patterns of support and tension. Pedagogy, in and out of school, plays an often mystified role in their articulations. Remaining educational/training autonomies and their hopes for participation in emancipatory practices and projects must be fashioned on these grounds.

Notes

1. The closest approximation to this is to sell the product before it is made—El Dorado! This is certainly one of the driving forces behind modern production technology and the sporadic arrival of post-Fordism: i.e., advance orders for cars, which are made only to specification and with a customer waiting. But it is much more difficult to sell cultural commodities before they are made; and once made, there are enormous dangers of the product staying in the warehouse. Negative and uncreative responses to the danger include market flooding and repetition: producing lots of items almost randomly in order to maximize the odds of producing at least one winner and repeating, ad nauseam, the formulas of the occasional winners, namely, the standardized genres and clichéd visual imagery that surround us. From here flow tendencies toward the much-discussed homogeneity of capitalist culture, toward the restriction of choice, and toward the leveling down to lowest common denominator. There are, however, countertendencies, which should not be underestimated, arising form the pressure to sell and to find new markets.

2. This point was suggested to me by Phil Corrigan. This chapter has benefited in numerous other ways from his detailed comments on draft versions.

3. There are of course rules for the consumption of cultural commodities, including possession of cash and, not least, concerning legal purchase and ownership and conformity with the requirements of copyright law. Compared with the norms and requirements surrounding the consumption of high-cultural items, these are at least explicit, visible, and simple and are frequently their own incitement to transgression.

4. Street drugs (marijuana, amphetamines, LSD, cocaine, crack, ecstasy) may be a particular kind of quintessential modern, "sticky," cultural commodity, the more so because of their illegality. It is reliably estimated that the United Kingdom is heading toward a plateau of drug-taking, in which about 50 percent of its young people will have some direct experience of drug-taking and 10–20 percent become regular, usually weekend, users. This follows the pattern in the United States very closely, though lagged by a few years. It is a mystery to professionals in the area why the trend has been so inexorable. It is certainly remarkable that drug use has risen in tandem with the rising satura-

tion of society by cultural commodities and the media. Possibly, young people's general experience of a commodity society makes them more open to the mysteries and promise of drugs, which are seen as similar to cultural commodities.

Drugs offer a maximum of suggestive openness with an unspecified but powerful internal dynamic. The pharmacological effect, "the buzz," offers all the metamorphoses of the cultural commodity but in a swift, programmed, and automatic way. There is no evident connection to other sites, histories, authorities, or dependencies (i.e., the inbuilt fetishistic nature of drugs). The act of taking drugs, therefore, helps to cut the individual and group loose from these anchors. At the same time, a powerful experience and meaning do seem to be on offer yet in a way that is "anchorable" by users in their own memories and experiences as well as in the rituals and practices of drug-taking itself.

No matter what the pharmacology of the particular drug, the common denominator seems to be a productive tension related to this double nature: powerful but unspecified external determinations and individual personalization of the actual experience. A common metaphor is of a film slipped onto the projector of the mind whose images and content are supplied by the user's own personal history, mental set, and setting. (Statistics here are drawn from Russell Newcombe, presentation at Young People and Drugs Conference, organized by the Youth Affairs Service of Wolverhampton Metropolitan Borough Council, October 21, 1994.)

5. This is not an attack on the avant-garde per se, only on its sociology (or lack of it) and on the irony of its frequent social misdirectedness. Avant-gardist practices certainly batter the illusions and auras of bourgeois culture, but they do not recognize, or adapt their messages for, other cultures. And they do not recognize or disdain the possibilities of these same *living* practices in different (subordinate) locations and contexts, so devaluing their *embodied* potentials for coherence and reconstruction.

References

Marx, Karl. 1957. *Capital.* Translated by Samuel Moore and Edward Aveling. London: Allen and Unwin.

Willis, Paul. 1981. *Learning to Labor.* New York: Columbia University Press.

———. 1983. "Cultural Production and Theories of Reproduction." In L. Barton and S. Walker, eds., *Race, Class, and Education.* London: Croom Helm.

———. Forthcoming. *Life as Art.* London: Polity.

Willis, Paul, et al. 1996 (1990). *Common Culture.* Boulder, Colo.: Westview Press.

Index